# Marvels Wonders & Extraordinary Manifestations

## OF THE GREATNESS OF OUR GOD

JERRY SAVELLE

Published by Jerry Savelle Ministries International
Crowly, Texas, U.S.A.
www.jerrysavelle.org

Unless noted otherwise, all Scripture is taken from the New King James Version®. Copyright© 1982 by Thomas Nelson. Used by permission. All rights reserved.

AMPC—Scripture quotations taken from the Amplified ® Bible (AMPC), Copyright © 1954, 1958, 1962, 1964, 1965, 1987 by The Lockman Foundation Used by permission. www.Lockman.org

Lamsa—HOLY BIBLE FROM THE ANCIENT EASTERN TEXT. Copyright © 1933 by A.J. Holman Co.; copyright © renewed 1961 by A.J. Holman Co. Copyright © 1939 by A.J. Holman Co.; copyright © renewed 1967 by A.J. Holman Co. Copyright © 1940 by A.J. Holman Co.; copyright renewed 1968 by A.J. Holman Co. Copyright © 19t7 by A.J. Holman Co. All rights reserved.

MSG—Scripture quotations are taken from THE MESSAGE, copyright © 1993, 2002, 2018 by Eugene H. Peterson. Used by permission of NavPress. All rights reserved. Represented by Tyndale House Publishers, Inc.

NIV—Scripture quotations marked (NIV) are taken from the Holy Bible, New International Version, NIV®. Copyright © 1973, 1978, 1984, 2011, by Biblica, Inc. ™ Used by permission of Zondervan. All rights reserved worldwide. www.zonderfan.com The "NIV" and "New International Version" are trademarks registered in the United States Patent and Trademark Office by Biblica, Inc. ™

NLT—Scripture quotations marked (NLT) are taken from the Holy Bible, New Living Translation, copyright ©1996, 2004, 2015 by Tyndale House Foundation. Used by permission of Tyndale House Publisher, Inc., Carol Stream, Illinois 60188. All rights reserved.

TPT—The Passion Translation®. Copyright © 2017 by Passion & Fire Ministries, Inc. Used by permission. All rights reserved. thePassionTranlation.com

Phillips—J.B. Phillips, "the new Testament in Modern English", 1962 edition, published by Harper Collins.

WYC—Wycliff Bible Copyright © 2001 by Terrence P. Noble.

© 2019 Jerry Savelle Ministries International. All rights reserved.
ISBN 978-1-939934-45-1

Rights for publishing this book outside the U.S.A or in non-English languages are administered by Jerry Savelle Ministries, an international not-for-profit ministry. For additional information, please visit jerrysavelle.org, or email info@jsmi.org, or write to Jerry Savelle Ministries International, PO Box 748, Crowley, TX 76036, U.S.A.
To order copies of this book and other resources in bulk quantities,
Please contact us at 1-817-297-3155.

# TABLE OF CONTENTS

CHAPTER 1 - *God's Wonders—Then and Now* ........................ 7

CHAPTER 2 - *A Sense of Admiration and Reverance* ............23

CHAPTER 3 - *Prepare for an Outpouring* ................................39

CHAPTER 4 - *We Are Heirs of Salvation* ................................55

CHAPTER 5 - *Angels on Assignment* ......................................69

CHAPTER 6 - *Angels in Our Financial Harvest* ......................83

CHAPTER 7 - *Wage the Good Warfare* ....................................99

CHAPTER 8 - *Prepared for the Harvest* ................................115

CHAPTER 9 - *Positioned for the Abundant Harvest* ............129

# PART 1
## God's Covenant of Wonders

*"I am making a covenant with you.
Before all your people I will do wonders never
before done in any nation in all the world."*
— Exodus 34:10 (NIV)

# CHAPTER 1
## God's Wonders—Then and Now

Not long after I surrendered my life to the Lord in 1969 and shut down my paint-and-body business to answer God's call on my life, I was driving an old Oldsmobile luxury sedan that I'd purchased after it had been wrecked. It looked like new after I rebuilt it; however, beneath the hood both the engine and transmission were nearly shot. The luxury had left that car a long time ago, but it was the only car Carolyn and I had when I went to work for Kenneth Copeland Evangelistic Association.

I remember getting up early to pray that the old sedan would start on the cold January morning I was scheduled to pick up Brother Copeland and take him to the airport. When I arrived at his house, I left the car running while I went to the front door to let him know I was there. I didn't dare turn off the engine because I didn't know if it would start again.

We got in the car, and I could see Brother Copeland's breath as he turned to me and said, "Turn on the heater, Jerry."

"It's on full blast right now," I replied.

One thing I'd learned about faith from Brother Copeland was that we are not to be moved by what we see, what we hear, or what we feel; we are to be moved only by the Word of God. So when he asked if the heater was really on I said, "Yes. Don't be moved by what you feel."

He was quiet for a few moments as he sat there shivering, and then he declared, "In the name of Jesus, I command this heater to work!" That heater came on, and within minutes it was so hot in the car that I had to turn it off.

I didn't know it at the time, but God was using that old Oldsmobile to teach me about one vital facet of His character: He is a wonder-working God. He had revealed Himself as the God of wonders to the children of Israel when He said to Moses, *"I am making a covenant with you. Before all your people I will do wonders never before done in any nation in all the world. The people you live among will see how awesome is the work that I, the Lord, will do for you"* (Exodus 34:10 NIV).

God was establishing this covenant in behalf of His people, those who already knew and worshiped Him as the God of Abraham, Isaac, and Jacob. Notice the reason for this covenant was not solely to perform wonders for the benefit of the children of Israel; it was so that others could see the awesome works of the Lord.

At the time God made this covenant, He had already brought the children of Israel out of captivity in Egypt. He had already inflicted plagues of gnats, flies, frogs, boils, hail, and locusts on Egypt. He had already led the Israelites as a cloud by day and a pillar of fire by night. He had already parted the Red Sea so that they could safely cross on dry ground, and then He drowned the Egyptian army that pursued them. Yet He made a covenant that He would do wonders never before done in any nation of the world.

Some may say, "Well, that's what He said to Moses and the children of Israel. What does that have to do with us?" The key word in Exodus 34:10 is *covenant*. God never breaks a covenant. People may break covenants, but God does not. The Bible says, For when God made a promise to Abraham, because He could swear by no one greater, He swore by Himself, saying, *"Surely blessing I will bless you, and multiplying I will multiply you." For men indeed swear by the greater, and an oath for confirmation is for them an end of all strife* (Hebrews 4:13–14, 16).

In the mind of God, His covenant is a sure thing. We've all watched courtroom dramas where witnesses take the stand and say, "I swear to tell the truth, the whole truth, and nothing but the truth, so help me God." What are they doing? They are swearing by a greater one. God couldn't swear by anyone greater than Himself, because He is the Most High God. So in essence what He said to Abraham was, "If I ever break My word to you, then I forfeit everything I have, because I swear by Myself." In other words, God laid the whole corporate structure of heaven on the line when He made this covenant of performing wonders.

The Bible goes on to say, *Thus God, determining to show more abundantly to the heirs of promise the immutability of His counsel, confirmed it by an oath, that by two immutable things, in which it is impossible for God to lie, we might have strong consolation, who have fled for refuge to lay hold of the hope set before us. This hope we have as an anchor of the soul, both sure and steadfast* (Hebrews 4:17-19).

The word *immutable* means "unchangeable." The two immutable things this scripture is talking about are His oath and His promise. When God takes an oath and He makes a promise, it is unchangeable. It is sure and steadfast, giving us hope. I've learned that every promise in the Word of God is unchangeable. That promise is reliable and steadfast. It may take some time for it to come to pass in my life, but if I dare to believe God's promise and refuse to let it go, it's only a matter of time before it happens.

I was still learning these Bible truths fifty years ago, and the Lord continued to use that old Oldsmobile to reveal Himself to me as the God of wonders. I needed new tires on the rear of that car, but I didn't have the money to pay for them. Brother Copeland had told me when I went to work for him that it was up to me to use my faith and to believe for my salary, which I was doing at the time I needed those tires. I was also learning to exercise my faith in God's promise that He would supply all of my needs.

I took the Olds to someone I knew who owned a service station and told him to put retreads on it; I had the money for those. When I went back to get the car, I was surprised to see two brand new tires on it. I told the owner I couldn't pay for new tires, and he said, "I was putting on the retreads when someone stopped and asked if that was Jerry Savelle's old car. When I said yes, the man said 'I don't want that boy having retreads. Put some new tires on the car and I'll pay for them—but don't tell him who did it.'"

When I drove away on those new tires, I wondered who had done that for me. I wondered for days. I wondered for weeks. Each time I got in, I wondered at what God had done. I was learning that anytime something happens that makes me wonder, then it is a wonder.

I continued to drive that wonder car for a time, to the point that I needed to replace the two front tires. I was heading north on I-35 from Fort Worth to Oklahoma City where I was scheduled to speak at a meeting; Carolyn and the girls were with me. We'd stopped at a drive-in for burgers, and when we pulled back onto the highway, a Firestone truck loaded with tires sped past us and disappeared over the hill. A few minutes later I noticed two moving objects in the road ahead, but I couldn't tell what they were. Carolyn said, "It looks like two tires." She was right.

Apparently they had fallen off the Firestone truck and were now rolling down the highway toward us. They eventually rolled into the ditch, where I stopped and picked up the brand new tires and then put them in the trunk of my car. There was no way I could catch the truck, so when I got to Oklahoma City, I called each of the four stores listed in the phone book to see if they'd lost any tires. No one had a report of missing tires. The last store manager I talked to said, "Sir, all I can tell you is that they're yours now. Take them." When I opened my trunk and examined the tires, I discovered they were the exact size I needed for my wonder car. I again wondered how this latest wonder had happened.

Carolyn and I were growing in our faith, and we started believing God for a better car. I knew a man who wanted to sell me his practically brand-new car with low mileage at a price below market value. I thought, *This has to be God*, so I said, "I'll take it, but I'm going to have to believe God to get me the money I need to pay you." The man said he would believe with me, and we shook hands. Some time passed, and he called me to ask if I had the money yet. I said, "I'm standing on Mark 11:24: '*Whatever things you ask when you pray, believe that you receive them, and you will have them.*'" He said he would stand in faith with me.

Several weeks passed, and he called again. "Have you gotten the money for that car yet?"

"I'm still standing on Mark 11:24," I said.

"Well, Jerry, I'm sorry to tell you, but I need to sell the car. I was hoping God would come through and make it happen for you by now, but I've got to sell this car."

I told him I understood, but when I hung up the phone my spirit fell. I thought, *Man, did I miss God here?* as I felt discouragement come upon me. Then I said, "Lord, what about this?"

He said, "A double-minded man is unstable in all his ways."

"Lord, did you hear the conversation? The man is selling the car."

Again He said, "A double-minded man is unstable in all his ways. Don't expect that man to receive anything from God." He was reminding me of James 1:7-8.

"Lord, You don't understand how we do things down here," I said. "The man is selling the car. I can't keep believing for it when he's selling it."

For the third time He answered, "A double-minded man is unstable in all his ways. Don't expect that man to receive anything from God."

So I said, "Are You telling me that You want me to continue to believe for that car even though the man is selling it?"

"A double-minded man ..."

I went to my wife and said, "Carolyn, the man is selling the car, but God told me a double-minded man is unstable and can't expect to receive anything from God, so I'm still believing that's my car!" She said she was in agreement with me.

Later that day the man called again and said, "Jerry, I owe you an apology. When I hung up the phone after talking with you, God got all over me. He said, 'You know that's Jerry Savelle's car, and you'd better do everything you can to see to it he gets it!' That's your car."

I said, "Yes, sir, it *is* my car," and then I told him what the Lord had said to me. The man told me to come over and get it, but I said, "No, not until I can pay cash for it."

That's when the man said, "Aren't you going to be making a trip soon?" I was actually getting ready to go to Arkansas to preach, with Carolyn and the girls accompanying me. I was determined to believe God that our old car would make it there and back. I told him about the Arkansas trip and he said, "I wouldn't be able to sleep if I knew you were on the highway with your family in that old car of yours. Come get the car!" I told him I would take the car—but I would return it when we got back from Arkansas.

We drove that car to Arkansas and back, and I can't tell you how much we appreciated having a safe and comfortable vehicle to travel in. I pulled up to the man's house to return the car, and he came out and asked if we enjoyed it. When I said yes, he said, "Well, it's yours."

"Yes, sir, I know it's mine," I said.

"Jerry, you're not listening. I said it's yours. While you were gone, somebody came and asked me about the car. I told him you had the car and were going to buy it, but you were believing for the money to pay cash for it. The man asked how much money you needed, and I told him. That's when he gave me the cash."

At that point the owner of the car handed me the title and said, "The car's yours!"

To this day I don't know who paid for that car. What I do know is that God performed yet another wonder in my life.

## How Did That Happen?

God is into doing things in a way that makes us pause and think, and then say, "I wonder how that happened? I wonder who did that?" He gets great pleasure in performing wonders for His children.

I also get great pleasure in doing things for people without their knowing I was involved. I enjoy telling the individual who helps make the transaction in someone else's behalf, "Don't tell them where this came from; just let them wonder." I've blessed a lot of people who don't have a clue that God used me to bless them.

Let's look again at the covenant God made with His people: *"I am making a covenant with you. Before all your people I will do wonders never before done in any nation in all the world. The people you live among will see how awesome is the work that I, the Lord, will do for you"* (Exodus 34:10 NIV). Some versions of the Bible use the word *marvels* instead of *wonders*. In Matthew's account of the gospel, we read this story about Jesus ministering to the people: As they went out, behold, they brought to Him a man, mute and demon-possessed. And when the demon was cast out, the mute spoke. And the multitudes marveled, saying, *"It was never seen like this in Israel!"* (Matthew 9:32–33).

Jesus and His disciples were in a boat on the sea when a great storm arose and covered the boat with waves. The Bible says, *But [Jesus] was asleep. Then His disciples came to Him and awoke Him, saying, "Lord, save us! We are perishing!" But He said to them, "Why are you fearful, O you of little faith?" Then He arose and rebuked the winds and the sea, and there was a great calm. So the men marveled, saying, "Who can this be, that even the winds and the sea obey Him?"* (Matthew 8:24–27).

When a paralytic lying on a bed was brought to Jesus, He said, *"Arise, take up your bed, and go to your house."* And he arose and departed to his house. Now when the multitudes saw it, they *marveled and glorified God* (Matthew 9:6–8). Notice what happens when people marvel over something God has done: God is glorified.

Some say we've already seen everything God can do, but I don't agree. There's still so much more that God has in store for us. The Bible says, *But as it is written: "Eye has not seen, nor ear heard, nor have entered into the heart of man the things which God has prepared for those who love Him"* (1 Corinthians 2:9). There are things our eyes haven't yet seen, our ears haven't yet heard, and our hearts haven't yet conceived. But God has already prepared them for us, and He is about to release them in our behalf.

The Message translation says, *"I will work wonders that have never been created in all the Earth"* (Exodus 34:10). The Amplified Bible says that those who see these wonders will be filled with awe. The word *awe* means "an overwhelming feeling of admiration and reverence." This is the result of God fulfilling His covenant, His solemn agreement. Psalms 89:34 tells us how God feels about His covenants: *My covenant I will not break, nor alter the word that has gone out of My lips. Once I have sworn by My holiness; I will not lie* (Psalms 89:34–35).

God's covenants are reliable; we can expect Him to back them. Through the prophet Isaiah, God said, *"So shall My word be that goes forth from My mouth; it shall not return to Me void, but it shall accomplish what I please, and it shall prosper in the thing for which I sent it* (Isaiah 55:11). The Message translation says, *"So will the words that come out of my mouth not come back empty-handed. They'll do the work I sent them to do, they'll complete the assignment I gave them."*

Every promise in the Word of God has an assignment to be fulfilled. Those who dare to believe the promise and hold fast to it will see God's assignment on the promise come to pass in their lives.

When God made the covenant of wonders with Moses, the children of Israel saw marvels, wonders, and extraordinary manifestations of God's greatness as they passed through the wilderness. When they entered into Canaan where the waters flowed abundantly, God healed them after they'd been bitten by fiery serpents. He divided the waters of the Jordan River. The Israelites saw the walls of Jericho fall down; they saw the sun and the moon stand still until God avenged them of their enemies. They saw things they had never before witnessed, which were obviously God's doing.

But God was not done with His covenant of wonders. Hundreds of years later the prophet Joel said, *Fear not, O land; be glad and rejoice: for the Lord will do great things* (Joel 2:21 KJV). The term great things indicates something beyond the usual.

### Beyond the Usual

We can expect to see God doing unusual things in the lives of believers; therefore, we must not limit Him to what we've already seen. We limit God when we think He can do something only the way we've seen Him move before. In essence, our limited thinking puts God in a box. We need to get Him out of the box and allow Him to do what He's already promised to do: demonstrate marvels, wonders, and extraordinary manifestations of His greatness.

We can learn a lesson from the story of Naaman, a commander in the army of the king of Syria. He was an honorable man, a mighty man of valor—and he was a leper. When he heard the prophet Elisha could heal him, Naaman went to see him.

> Then Naaman went with his horses and chariot, and he stood at the door of Elisha's house. And Elisha sent a messenger to him, saying, "Go and wash in the Jordan seven times, and your flesh shall be restored to you, and you shall be clean." But Naaman became furious, and went away and said, "Indeed, I said to myself, 'He will surely come out to

me, and stand and call on the name of the Lord his God, and wave his hand over the place, and heal the leprosy.' Are not the Abanah and the Pharpar, the rivers of Damasucs, better than the waters of Israel? Could I not wash in them and be clean?" So he turned and went away in a rage. And his servants came near and spoke to him, and said, "My father, if the prophet had told you to do something great, would you not have done it? How much more then, when he says to you, 'Wash, and be clean'?" So he went down and dipped seven times in the Jordan, according to the saying of the man of God; and his flesh was restored like the flesh of a little child, and he was clean (2 Kings 5:9–14).

Naaman had already made up his mind how God was going to heal him. As a result of his limited human thinking, he walked away from the miracle he needed. Were it not for his servants speaking words of wisdom to him, his healing would not have manifested. He would have missed God's wonder.

Like Namaan, believers often think God will "surely" answer their prayers in a certain way that they come up with. We need to let God be God; He doesn't need our help. God was fulfilling His covenant of wonders before we were ever born. If we could have made something happen, we would already have done so. Our job is to trust Him and obey His instructions.

God said, *"And I will show wonders in the heavens and in the earth"* (Joel 2:20). From the days of Moses to the book of Joel, God spoke about doing wonders; His covenant has not ceased. When God shows a wonder, we see things occur that are beyond the usual. I define a *wonder* as "something unfamiliar, unexplainable and could only happen by the hand of God."

God has shown His wonders to me many times throughout my ministry. I can never explain how He did what He did; I just know

He did it. For instance, a few years ago I took a commercial flight to Baltimore, where I was scheduled to preach. I had sown my airplane into another ministry, as I'd done numerous times before at the Lord's leading; however, this time I wasn't believing for my next airplane. I'd reasoned it would be good to slow down a bit and spend time with my family and enjoy the fruit of my labor. In my thinking, I didn't need another airplane—I was done with aviation.

I'd just returned to my Baltimore hotel room after preaching and was hanging my suit in the closet when I heard the Lord say, "At what time did I tell you that you can fulfill what you're called to do without your own airplane?"

"You didn't," I answered.

"Didn't I tell you back in 1969 when you first surrendered your life to Me that you wouldn't be able to fulfill what I've called you to do without airplanes in your ministry? Didn't I also tell you I didn't want you to ever borrow money for airplanes but you were to believe to pay cash for them?"

"Yes, Sir," I said.

"Then whose decision was it not to believe for your next airplane?"

"Apparently it was my decision."

The Lord said, "Then let me ask you this about your calling: Are you done? Are you through?"

"No, Sir, I'm not through," I said.

"If you're not through, then how can you fulfill what I've called you to do without airplanes in your ministry now?"

"Apparently I can't. I stand corrected; consider me back on faith for my next airplane."

I had no idea that at that precise time God was working behind the scenes in another nation. One of my partners in Australia had sold a business and sent a check to our Ministry. It arrived in Fort Worth while I was in Baltimore.

When I got home, I told Carolyn that I was back on my faith

for my next airplane. She said, "I knew being without your own airplane wouldn't last long." When I went to the ministry office, I learned that this partner in Australia had sent a check for $500,000, along with a note that the money was for my airplane. That partner had never heard me say I was done with aviation; he just heard God say, "Send him half a million dollars."

Soon afterward I got a call from Keith and Phyllis Moore. Brother Keith said, "Brother Jerry, the last time we talked, you said you didn't think you were going to own airplanes anymore. Are you sure about that?" I told him what had happened in Baltimore and that I was back in faith again for my next airplane. Brother Keith said, "I didn't think that was what God wanted when you said it, but I didn't want to say anything at the time. But Phyllis and I are believing for our next airplane, and God told us to give you the one we are flying now."

When he flew the plane to me in Fort Worth and we took possession, Brother Keith said, "It's a good airplane, but soon, you may need to look into some new avionics." When I researched the cost of the avionics, I learned it would take about $500,000 to do the job correctly. God had supplied the money for the upgrades before I ever got the airplane. That's our God—the God of wonders!

## He Is Forever the God of Wonders

God spoke through the prophet Malachi, saying, *"For I am the Lord, I do not change"* (Malachi 3:6); therefore, we know that if He was the God of wonders in both the Old and New Testaments, then He is the God of wonders today.

The psalmist affirmed Him as the God of wonders when he penned these words: *Declare His glory among the nations, His wonders among all peoples* (Psalms 96:3–4) and *Oh, give thanks to the Lord of lords! For His mercy endures forever: to Him who alone does great wonders* (Psalms 136:3–4).

In the New Testament we find the account of the day of Pentecost. After the hundred and twenty were filled with the Holy Ghost, Peter stood up and said, *"But this is what was spoken by the prophet Joel: 'And on My menservants and on My maidservants I will pour out My Spirit in those days; and they shall prophesy. I will show wonders in heaven above'"* (Acts 2:18–19). Clearly, God's covenant of wonders didn't end with Moses. It didn't end with Joel, and it didn't end on the day of Pentecost. God is forever the God of wonders, keeping covenant with those of every generation who choose to believe.

We can also see the account of wonders being shown through the hands of the apostles as God formed the early Church:

> And through the hands of the apostles many signs and wonders were done among the people. And they were all in one accord in Solomon's Porch. And believers were increasingly added to the Lord, multitudes of both men and women, so that they brought the sick out into the streets and laid them on beds and couches, that at least the shadow of Peter passing by might fall on some of them. Also a great multitude gathered from the surrounding cities to Jerusalem, bringing sick people and those who were tormented by unclean spirits, and they were all healed (Acts 5:12, 14–16).

Here we see a great multitude of people, many who were sick or tormented by unclean spirits, and all were healed—even those who were merely exposed to Peter's shadow. The book of Acts goes on to say, *And Stephen, full of faith and power, did great wonders and signs among the people* (Acts 6:8). Speaking of the things that happened in his own ministry, the apostle Paul said, *In mighty signs and wonders, by the power of the Spirit of God, so that from Jerusalem and round about to Illyricum I have fully preached the gospel of Christ* (Romans 15:19).

I remember being in a Southern California mall one day with Carolyn and the girls as they went shopping. I told them I planned to enjoy some window-shopping while they went to their favorite stores and that then we'd meet for lunch. I'd been walking for a while, going from window to window, sometimes zigzagging from one side of the mall to the other, when someone came up behind me and laid a hand on my shoulder. A woman then declared, "I knew it was you! I knew it was you!"

I turned to face her and said, "It's me."

She said, "I've been sick, and the doctors don't know what's wrong with me. I was lying in my bed this morning, and God said, 'Get up and follow the light, and you'll receive your healing.' When I asked Him where to go, He told me to go to the mall. So I came here and stood at the end of the mall and looked around. When I saw this light moving from one store to the other, crisscrossing the mall, I took off running. I knew when I touched the light, I'd be healed."

And God healed her instantly.

I can't say that every time I go to the mall a miracle like this happens, but it happened that time as God showed a wonder in behalf of that woman. We limit God when we think He is bound to accomplish things in a certain way. We know God is already planning to reveal wonders in our lives, things that are unfamiliar and unexplainable, but it is up to us to be in position to receive His wonders.

We position ourselves to receive His wonders by lining up our words with His Word. We need to get rid of words like these: "That's impossible." "I've never heard of anything like that." "There's no way." "I can't believe that." We need to stop this kind of talk and instead declare, "The God of wonders is going to do mighty things in my life. This is my time for marvels, wonders, and extraordinary manifestations of the greatness of my God!"

Again, God has made a covenant that gives us access to His

wonders. The Word of God says, *He's God, our God, in charge of the whole earth. And he remembers, remembers his Covenant—for a thousand generations he's been as good as his word* (Psalms 105:7–8 MSG). The Amplified Bible says, *He is [earnestly] mindful of His covenant and forever it is imprinted on His heart* (verse 8). For God to no longer show marvels, wonders, and extraordinary manifestations of His greatness, He would have to break His own Word, which is imprinted on His heart and He will never do that.

The Bible describes God this way: *Who does great things, and unsearchable, marvelous things without number* (Job 5:8). The Message translation says, *After all, he's famous for great and unexpected acts; there's no end to his surprises.* God's wonders will take us by surprise. I know this is true because it happens to me all the time. The Bible says, *And all these blessings shall come upon you and overtake you, because you obey the voice of the Lord your God* (Deuteronomy 28:2). Blessings will come upon us and take us by surprise.

Moses said, *"Who is like You, O Lord, among the gods? Who is like You, glorious in holiness, fearful in praises, doing wonders?"* (Exodus 15:11). The Message translation says, *Who compares with you ... wonder-working God?* God is forever the God of wonders for those who receive His Word by faith. The Bible says, *For indeed the gospel was preached to us as well to them; but the word which they heard did not profit them, not being mixed with faith in those who heard it* (Hebrews 4:2). Notice there were people who heard what God had to say, but they didn't mix their faith with what they heard.

I invite you to join me today and boldly declare, "The God of wonders is showing His wonders, marvels, and extraordinary manifestations of His greatness in my life—I receive it!"

# CHAPTER 2
## A Sense of Admiration and Reverance

Shortly after I first came to the Lord, Carolyn and I attended a Bible study in the home of a couple that went to our church. I remember one night in particular being seated in a circle of chairs in the couple's living room when the man leading the study said, "Let's all pray in the Spirit for a while."

After we'd prayed for a few minutes, he asked if there was anyone visiting for the first time, and a man raised his hand. The visitor introduced himself and told us he was from another country. When the Bible study leader finished his teaching from the Word, he said, "Let's all pray in the Spirit again." We prayed for only a few minutes before the visitor stopped, opened his eyes wide, and looked at the group leader who was still praying in the Spirit.

The visitor said, "I know what you are saying. You are speaking in my native tongue!"

Now our study leader was praying in tongues; he didn't understand what he was saying. However, the words he was speaking were in the visitor's language. The leader said, "If you understand what I'm saying, tell us what I just said."

The visitor said, "I came to the meeting tonight to ask you to pray for my wife who is back home in our country and is very ill. She is not doing well, and I was told she might not live. But I just heard you speak in my native tongue and say, 'Don't worry about your wife. I'm healing her right now!'"

Our Bible study leader had never before met the man who had come for prayer nor known the man's wife was dying. But

God knew—and He showed that man a wonder. In fact, we all wondered at the graciousness of God and His amazing ability to speak to that man.

I was young in the Lord and had never seen anything like that happen before, but experiencing God's wonder that night had a powerful impact on me: I left the meeting with a newfound sense of admiration and reverence for God

I've witnessed God's wonders consistently in my life and ministry over the past fifty years, but I believe we are now seeing His wonders, marvels, and extraordinary manifestations of greatness with increased frequency. The Word of God alone carries power when it is preached; however, the Word that is accompanied by signs and wonders, miracles and marvels, and manifestations of God's greatness brings forth in people a profound sense of admiration and reverence for God—just as it first did for me in 1969.

When people see something happen that could not have occurred in the natural, they know they've just witnessed a miracle from the God of wonders. My wife often tells the story about the woman who played the piano at the church Carolyn attended while growing up. At the time, this woman, Anna Jeannne Price, was one of the greatest pianists in the country. As a child she'd longed to play the piano, but her family had very little money. God supernaturally provided a piano, and because she babysat for the young Van Cliburn whose mother was a piano teacher, she exchanged babysitting services for piano lessons. As an adult, Anna Jeanne amazed people with what she could do with a piano.

I was with Carolyn one night at a Holy Ghost meeting at the church when the presence and glory of God manifested in a powerful way. Anna Jeannne was playing and singing a fast, upbeat song when the power of God came upon her. She stood up, raised her hands, and danced until her hair shook loose from her bun—while the piano continued to play!

We all looked back and forth from Anna Jeanne to the piano in wide-eyed wonder. Some may say, "That's impossible. I don't believe it!" But I was there, and I saw it. To this day I still wonder how God made that happen; that's why it's called a wonder.

In chapter 1 we studied God's covenant of wonders, in which He told Moses, *"Before all your people I will do wonders never before done in any nation in all the world"* (Exodus 34:10 NIV). The prophet Joel declared that the Lord would do "great things," which Peter referred to when explaining to the multitudes in Jerusalem the supernatural manifestations of the Holy Spirit on the Day of Pentecost. We learned the term *great things* implies "beyond the usual"; this is exactly what Carolyn and I experienced in the beginning of my walk with the Lord.

Brother Copeland was preaching at our church, and our eighteen-month-old daughter Terri was in the nursery while Carolyn and I attended the meeting. When Terri crawled beneath a rocking chair, the tips of two of her fingers were severed. The nursery worker brought her to us in the auditorium, where Brother Copeland immediately stepped down from the platform and prayed for her.

The plastic surgeon who treated Terri was a Buddhist. He said all he could do was a skin graft and that her fingers would never be normal for the rest of her life. Carolyn and I refused to agree with this report. We declared, "No, our God is going to restore our baby's fingers!" The surgeon told us it was impossible for her fingers to be normal, and said we shouldn't get our hopes up. I said, "Sir, we already have our hopes up because we know in whom we believe. Our God is not going to disappoint us."

When we took Terri back to him to have the dressing removed, he was careful to unwind the gauze. Suddenly he took a step back and said, "My god!" I asked what was the matter, and he said, "The fingers are back! The nails are back! My god, this is a miracle!"

I said, "No, sir, not your god—my God did this!" The God of wonders worked in our behalf.

When God made the covenant of wonders with Moses, He said, *"The people you will live among will see how awesome is the work that I, the Lord, will do for you"* (Exodus 34:10 NIV). Notice it says the people you will live among will see. That doctor saw what the God of wonders did that day. Although Carolyn and I did not stay in contact with him following the restoration of Terri's fingertips, we learned several years later that both the doctor and his wife were born again as a result of that miracle.

God is indeed still the God of wonders. He is still doing great things—beyond the usual. The Bible says, *Who is like You, O Lord, among the gods? Who is like You, glorious in holiness, fearful in praises, doing wonders?* (Exodus 15:11). The Message translation says, *Who compares with you among the gods, O God? Who compares with you in power, in holy majesty, in awesome praises, wonder-working God?* Our God is still the wonder-working God!

In the book of Job, once again, we find a verse that has become one of my favorite descriptions of God: *Who does great things, and unsearchable, marvelous things without number* (Job 5:9). The Message translation says, *After all, he's famous for great and unexpected acts; there's no end to his surprises.* God's wonders will take us by surprise. I know this is true because it happens to me all the time. In Chapter 1, I shared that the Bible says, *And all these blessings shall come upon you and overtake you, because you obey the voice of the Lord your God* (Deuteronomy 28:2). One of the literal Hebrew meanings for the word overtake in this verse is "to take by surprise." Blessings will come upon us and take us by surprise.

### God Is Famous for Surprises

I love surprises. It's not that I don't expect God to show wonders in my life; rather, I never know how He is going to do them. Jesus demonstrated this principle in the following familiar story from the book of Matthew:

> When they had come to Capernaum, those who received temple tax came to Peter and said, "Does your Teacher not pay the temple tax?"
> He said, "Yes."
> And when he had come into the house, Jesus anticipated him, saying, "What do you think Simon?" From whom do the kings of the earth take customs or taxes, from their sons or from strangers?"
> Peter said to Him, "From strangers."
> Jesus said to him, "Then the sons are free. Nevertheless, lest we offend them, go to the sea, cast in a hook, and take the fish that comes up first. And when you have opened its mouth, you will find a piece of money; take that and give it to them for Me and you" (Matthew 17:24–27).

Peter was a fisherman by trade before he became a disciple of Jesus. I'm confident in saying that in all the years Peter had been in the business, he'd never caught a fish with money in its mouth. Had he done so, he would have said, "Oh, Jesus, thanks for reminding me. That's the way I pay my taxes every year: I go fishing and find a fish with my tax money in its mouth." No! Peter was surprised when he caught that fish.

Now consider all the fish in that body of water that day and answer this question: which fish knew it would be the "first fish" Jesus spoke about? Fish are different from people; fish obey God. What if God told a particular individual to bless somebody, but the individual God spoke to didn't listen and obey? This happened to me one time, years ago when I was working for Brother Copeland.

It was my job to load and unload the equipment from the vehicle and drive it to and from the meetings. One afternoon as we were preparing to leave for a meeting the following morning, the Lord told me He wanted me to take some money to a particular minister. I didn't have a lot of money on me at the time, but I said,

"Lord, as soon as I finish and get in the car I'll do that." Later I finished packing and forgot about what the Lord had said to me.

That evening He said, "I told you earlier today to take that money to the minister."

I said, "Lord, I am so sorry. I forgot, but I'll do it first thing in the morning before I leave town."

I went to sleep and then got up the next morning and headed out of town. I'd driven all the way to Texarkana when I heard the Lord say, "I thought you were going to take that money to him before you left town."

"Lord, I am so sorry; I forgot again."

He said, "Forget it, I'll find somebody else."

Now if He'd just left it at that, I'd have felt bad enough. But then He said, "The next time you have a need, if I have to talk to two or three people before that need is met don't complain—you set the precedent." When God gives us instructions of any kind, we should be quick to obey. Our obedience may be the key to God's planned surprise for someone else. I immediately called that Minister and apologized and had my wife take the money to him.

Imagine Peter's surprise at the way the tax money came. He didn't know what was going to happen, but when Jesus spoke, the fish heard. I can imagine every fish in that lake hunting for money, each wanting to be the first fish Peter caught.

Another example of God's surprises is the way He fed a multitude of people who had come to hear Jesus preach in a deserted area belonging to the city called Bethsaida.

> When the day began to wear away, the twelve came and said to Him, "Send the multitude away, that they may go into the surrounding towns and country, and lodge and get provisions; for we are in a deserted place here."
>
> But He said to them, "You give them something to eat."
>
> And they said, "We have no more than five loaves and two

fish, unless we go and buy food for all these people." For there were about five thousand men.

Then He said to His disciples, "Make them sit down in groups of fifty." And they did so, and made them all sit down.

Then He took the five loaves and the two fish, and looking up to heaven, He blessed and broke them, and gave them to the disciples to set before the multitude. So they all ate and were filled, and twelve baskets of the leftover fragments were taken up by them (Luke 9:10–16).

Don't you just know God was saying, "Surprise!" He is famous for surprises. Something similar once happened to our International Director, Joe McCroskey, when he and a team were ministering in Tanzania. The team had provided a great quantity of food to feed the poor; however, more people showed up than expected. The food was almost gone, yet there were many more people waiting to be fed. Joe and the team prayed, "Jesus, You multiplied the food before; do it again!" It turned out they fed everyone who came and even had food left over. It was a modern-day wonder.

Jesus constantly surprised His disciples, who declared, *What manner of man is this, that even the winds and the sea obey him!* (Matthew 8:27 KJV). Imagine how baffled they were the day He announced to them He was going away. They'd been with him for three years; He'd met their every need in ways they couldn't have dreamed possible. Then, all of a sudden, they learned He was going away.

Jesus went on to say, *"I tell you the truth, anyone who believes in me will do the same works I have done, and even greater works, because I am going to be with the Father"* (John 14:12 NLT). But how would believers be able to do the greater works Jesus spoke about? Because He was going to the Father, where He would have no limitations after He sent the Holy Spirit: *"And I will ask the*

*Father, and he will give you another Advocate, who will never leave you. He is the Holy Spirit, who leads into all truth"* (John 14:16–17 NLT).

In the day in which Matthew, Mark, Luke, and the others lived with Jesus, He could only be *with* them. But we are believers who have the Holy Spirit not only *with* us, but *in* us as well. We can *expect* to experience God's marvels, wonders, and extraordinary manifestations of His greatness everywhere we go and for as long as we live!

The apostle John said at the conclusion of his epistle, *And there are also many other things that Jesus did, which if they were written one by one, I suppose that even the world itself could not contain the books that would be written* (John 21:25). This means that everything recorded in the Bible doesn't cover everything Jesus did while He was living and ministering on Earth. The Bible gives us only a taste of the wonderful works He did.

I like the way Psalms 40:5 reads in the Amplified Bible: *Many, O Lord my God, are the wonderful works which You have done, and Your thoughts toward us; no one can compare with You! If I should declare and speak of them, they are too many to be numbered.* John said everything Jesus did couldn't be listed, and David said God's works are too many to be numbered. It sounds to me like the Bible is certainly correct when it says that God is famous for doing great and unexpected acts and that His surprises cannot be numbered.

Jesus is not a retired preacher or miracle worker. He is still in the miracle worker, and the Holy Spirit is still with us. God's marvels, wonders, and extraordinary manifestations of His greatness have not ended. They didn't end with David; they didn't end with Jesus; they didn't end with John or Paul. And I truly believe that God's best is yet to come—in ways that will always surprise us!

### God's Limitless Works

I've seen a lot in the fifty years I've been in the ministry. I've experienced God's miracles and countless manifestations of His greatness—but I haven't yet seen it all.

According to Job 5:9, *God's deeds are beyond human investigation and reasoning.* The Lamsa Bible says, *God does great things without limit.* In other words, God's works are limitless. Looking again at Paul's words to the church in Corinth, we see that *"eye has not seen, nor ear heard, nor have entered into the heart of man the things which God has prepared for those who love Him"* (1 Corinthians 2:9). Paul was quoting the words of Isaiah from the Old Testament; however, he went on to say, *But God has revealed them to us through His Spirit* (verse 10).

What would be the purpose of God preparing these things—these marvels, wonders, and extraordinary manifestations of His greatness—if He wasn't going to manifest them? Why would He prepare these things for those who love Him, and then not allow them to be experienced? Why would He allow us to get our hopes up, and then not be true to His Word?

Have you ever had someone tell you something that builds up your hope, but then that person didn't come through with what they had promised? That's not the way God operates. If God has prepared things for those who love Him—things our eyes have not seen, our ears have not heard about, and our hearts have not conceived—then those things are on the way. And I plan to be a recipient of them.

Through the prophet Jeremiah, God said, *For I know the thoughts that I think toward you, says the Lord, thoughts of peace and not of evil, to give you a future and a hope* (Jeremiah 29:11). God has made plans for me, and He has made plans for you. I expect God's plan for me to be fulfilled and in my lifetime. How about you? God plans to give us the futures we have hoped for; however, it is up to us to stay in faith and never to give up on His plan or His Word. The NIV Bible says that God's plans are to prosper us. The word *prosper* means "to succeed; to become strong; to thrive; to flourish." That's God's plan for our lives. To *succeed* indicates things will turn out well. Joseph was a man who experienced what may have looked like failure in his life after his brothers sold him into slavery in Egypt. However, he became the second most powerful man in Egypt next to Pharaoh. Joseph later said to his brothers, *But as for you, you meant evil against me; but God meant it for good"* (Genesis 50:20). God can turn the evil things Satan does in our lives into something good.

God knows the end from the beginning. As far as He's concerned, no situation is over until He says it's over—and He never says it's over until we win! His marvelous works in our behalf are without limit. His plans for us are not for evil. If the enemy plans something evil against us, God will turn it into something good. He's got us covered, for the Word says, *And we know that all things work together for good to those who love God, to those who are called according to His purpose* (Romans 8:28).

Divine providence always overcomes evil intentions. This is one of the reasons James says we are to count it all joy when we fall into various trials, tests, and temptations (see James 1:2). Why should we count it all joy when being tested and tried? We can count it all joy because providence always overcomes evil intentions. In other words, God's not done yet.

If you are in a situation that seems to have gone wrong or something adverse has happened that you hadn't expected, I can tell you with certainty that God will turn around what the enemy meant for your harm. Don't ever give up on God and the limitless works He has in store for you.

I've had God do marvelous things for me in the past, and I expect Him to do them in the future; however, I've learned not to expect Him to do something exactly the same way each time. He is God, so I let Him be God. He has been showing His wondrous works for a long time, and He has ways of showing them that we couldn't dream up in a thousand years. God's wonders in my life have oftentimes utilized the most least-expected people. I've had Him meet significant financial needs in my life through individuals who appeared not to have two quarters to rub together. We can't look at everyone through only our natural eyes.

When God sent Samuel the prophet to Jesse's house to anoint the next king of Israel, the prophet asked Jesse to bring all of his sons before him. Jesse called all of his sons except the youngest and smallest, David, whom Jesse left in the field to tend the sheep because he didn't think David would be the one. Each of Jesse's sons passed before Samuel, but then something interesting happened.

> And Samuel said to Jesse, "The Lord has not chosen these ... Are all the young men here?" Then he said, "There remains yet the youngest, and there he is, keeping the sheep."
> And Samuel said to Jesse, "Send and bring him. For we will not sit down till he comes here." So he sent and brought him in. Now he was ruddy, with bright eyes, and good-looking. And the Lord said, "Arise, anoint him; for this is the one!" Then Samuel took the horn of oil and anointed him in the midst of his brothers; and the Spirit of the Lord came upon David from that day forward (1 Samuel 16:10–13).

God doesn't look at the outward appearance. If I'd had to select someone to meet a need in my life, I'd have missed it many times because I would have chosen someone who looked as if they had the ability to do so. But this is not always how God works.

## God Doesn't Consider Appearance

When Samuel first saw Jesse's older son Eliab, he thought surely the young man was God's anointed one. But the Lord said to Samuel, *"Do not look at his appearance or at his physical stature ... For the Lord does not see as man sees; for man looks at the outward appearance, but the Lord looks at the heart"* (1 Samuel 16:7). God demonstrated this truth to me in a powerful way in a small Texas town in the 1970s.

I was believing for my first airplane, but it was not something I talked about publicly; I'd told only a handful of people. I was invited to preach at a church in Andrews, Texas; however, when I arrived and the pastor learned I was neither licensed nor ordained with his church's denomination, he wouldn't allow me to speak. At the time I didn't know a thing about religious politics or that situations like that could happen in a church.

One of the deacons came to me and said, "Brother Jerry, if I can find a place to have a meeting, will you stay?" I told him I'd come to preach and that's exactly what I'd do if he could find a place. The only vacant space in town was an abandoned laundromat on Main Street, which had been closed for a while. The deacon located the owner, who agreed to let us use it for the next three days.

We pushed all the washers up against one wall and most of the dryers against another wall. We started the meetings that night with Carolyn and me, our two daughters, and two of my staff and the deacon and his wife in attendance. That was our crowd the first night.

The deacon had brought a Kentucky Fried Chicken bucket to use when we received the offering. When we passed the bucket, I could hear the coins hitting the heavy cardboard bottom. Needless to say, it didn't take long to count the offering that night.

The plan was to do three services each day for the next two days. The first morning at ten o'clock we had the same crowd as the night before—plus one other person. But I preached as if the house were full. My topic was "The Word of Faith." That afternoon we had several more people, and at the evening meeting the crowd had grown to about two dozen people.

I was preaching again on faith the following morning when I looked through the big windows of the storefront and saw a pickup truck pull into one of the parking spaces in front of the laundromat. A large man wearing bib overalls stepped out of the truck, removed his straw hat, and then came through the door into our meeting. I figured he'd sit down, but he didn't. He walked directly toward me.

Unable to ignore him, I said, "Sir, would you like to take a seat?"

"No, I wouldn't," he said, and then added, "My name is Oop." It was clear he was a country boy.

"Okay, Mr. Oop, would you like to take a seat?" I asked.

He said, "No I wouldn't. God sent me here. I'm not educated; I can't read or write, but I can hear the voice of God. That's how I live—I hear God."

I had no idea where the conversation was going.

He continued, "I was out on my tractor plowing my field when I heard God say, 'There's a young man preaching in the laundry mat in Andrews and he needs an airplane. Go help him.' Are you him?"

I thought, *There can't be two of us preaching at a laundry mat in Andrews*—so I said yes.

"God told me to bring you some money for that airplane," he said. "I'm going to give you some money, and then I'm going to leave, and you'll never see me again unless God tells me. I don't do anything except what God tells me." Then he pulled handfuls of money out of the pockets in his overalls and piled it at my feet. When he was done, he put his straw hat back on his head, walked out the front door, got into his truck, and then drove away.

I looked at Carolyn and said, "Did this really just happen?" She told me to look at my feet, where the money Oop had pulled from his overalls was still piled. All I could think was, *Did this really happen?*

Although Oop's surprise provision didn't cover the cost of an airplane, it marked the birth of my airplane fund. I considered those funds to be the first manifestation of what I refer to as "the law of progression" as defined by Jesus: *"First the blade, then the head, after that the full grain in the head"* (Mark 4:28). When Oop obeyed God, the financial barrier between me and that airplane was broken. Those who were with me that day experienced a renewed sense of admiration and reverence for the greatness of our God.

In my wildest dreams I couldn't have imagined God would use someone named Oop to help me in getting my first airplane. On my best day of "helping God," I couldn't have imagined saying, "Okay, God, how are we going to get this airplane? Lord, how about You send somebody with some money? And then have him say, 'God told me to bring you some money.' Oh, and then have his name be Oop." I would never have come up with that in a million years. Yet to manifest His provision in a way far beyond the usual, God used a man whose outer appearance could have caused him to be overlooked but whose heart was faithful and obedient.

It wasn't long after this encounter that my first debt-free airplane manifested, but it all started with a man named Oop.

I like The Message translation of James 1:2: *Consider it a sheer gift, friends, when tests and challenges come at you from all sides. You know that under pressure, your faith-life is forced into the open and shows its true colors.* In other words, we're not to give up when we're under pressure. That's when God is most likely to bring a surprise, when He's most likely to turn what the enemy meant for bad into something good.

The Bible says, *Now thanks be to God who always leads us in triumph in Christ* (2 Corinthians 2:14). When we go through a trial, all we see is the trial; however, God sees us in the process of moving in triumph. This is why it is so important that we stay in faith and never give up. God is a wonder-working God. He is the God of surprises. The Bible says, *Now this is the confidence that we have in Him, that if we ask anything according to His will, He hears us. And if we know that He hears us, whatever we ask, we know that we have the petitions that we have asked of Him* (1 John 5:14–15). The Holy Spirit drew my attention to this verse, and then inspired me to write the following petition. I invite you to join me in declaring it out loud.

> Heavenly Father, in the name of Jesus, You are the God of the breakthrough; You are the God of the turnaround. You take what the devil means for bad, and You turn it into something good. You are good and the source of all good.
>
> Your Word declares that no weapon formed against us shall prosper and that triumph over opposition is the heritage of the servants of the Lord. You're the God who preserves and the God who vindicates the faithful. You're the God who leads us into victory in every transition and in every changing season of our lives. You are the God who teaches us to profit, the God who restores everything Satan has stolen from us.
>
> We have nothing to fear because You are for us; You are by our side. And if our God be for us, then no one can successfully be our enemy. You will not abandon us in our trouble, and You will not allow our adversary to prevail over us. Your goodness awaits us, and we wait on You; we will not waver.
>
> We now thank You in advance because we know that our God reigns; our God will not allow us to fail. We expect Your goodness, and we rejoice in Your loving kindness—in Jesus' name!

# CHAPTER 3
## Prepare for an Outpouring

Once, when Oral Roberts was in my home, I had a conversation with this great man who had been both a friend and mentor to me for many years. When I asked him what the Lord had most recently been speaking to him, he didn't hesitate before responding. "Jerry," he said, "the Lord spoke to me and told me, 'Oral, if you thought you saw signs, wonders, and miracles under the big tent, you haven't seen anything yet. They're coming back big time!'"

Of course, the Lord was referring to the tent crusades Brother Roberts had held during the late 1940s and 1950s, in which crowds of up to twelve thousand people came to hear the preacher from Oklahoma talk about Jesus and then pray for their healing. The miracles that happened during the early crusades are well documented; however, when Brother Roberts broadcast his first primetime live TV healing service in 1955, people could see for themselves the manifestations of God's greatness through the hands of the healing evangelist.

I believe God is preparing us for a mighty move and outpouring that will involve marvels, wonders, and extraordinary manifestations of His greatness. In today's world it takes more than just a good sermon to get people's attention. When nonbelievers see something happen beyond natural explanation, they are drawn to God.

The Bible says, *Then a great multitude followed [Jesus], because they saw His signs which He performed on those who were diseased* (John 6:2). Jesus said, *"And these signs will follow those who believe: In My name they will cast out demons; they will speak with new tongues; they will take up serpents; and if they drink anything deadly, it will by no means hurt them; they will lay hands on the sick, and they will recover"* (Mark 16:17–18). The passage goes on to say, *And they went out and preached everywhere, the Lord working with them and confirming the word through accompanying signs* (verse 20). Anytime the Lord is working with an individual, signs, wonders, and miracles will take place.

It's interesting that God's miracles don't always occur the way people expect. Jesus experienced this issue when He was in a house teaching a group of people that included some of the religious Pharisees and teachers of the law.

> And the power of the Lord was present to heal them. Then behold, men brought on a bed a man who was paralyzed, whom they sought to bring in and lay before Him. And when they could not find how they might bring him in, because of the crowd, they went up on the housetop and let him down with his bed through the tiling into the midst before Jesus.
>
> When He saw their faith, He said to him, "Man, your sins are forgiven you."
>
> And the scribes and the Pharisees began to reason, saying, "Who is this who speaks blasphemies? Who can forgive sins but God alone?"
>
> But when Jesus perceived their thoughts, He answered and said to them, "Why are you reasoning in your hearts? Which is easier, to say, 'Your sins are forgiven you,' or to say, 'Rise up and walk'? But that you may know the Son of Man has power on earth to forgive sins"—He said to the man who was paralyzed, "I say to you, arise, take up your bed, and go to your house."
>
> Immediately he rose up before them, took up what he had been lying on, and departed to his own house, glorifying God. And they were all amazed, and they glorified God and

were filled with fear, saying, "We have seen strange things today!" (Luke 5:17–25).

Notice that the people said they had seen strange things- They'd seen was a marvel, a wonder, an extraordinary manifestation of God's greatness. To many people the miracle was strange; to others it was wonderful. Either way, what happened that day could only be attributed to God.

I believe God plans to close out this Church age with an outpouring of marvels, wonders, and extraordinary manifestations for this reason: it is His will that all men be saved. The Word of God says that *He is not willing that any should perish but that all should come to repentance* (2 Peter 3:9). For multitudes to come to Christ in these last days, it will require the preaching of the Word and signs that follow. But it is up to us to prepare ourselves if we want to experience all God has for us in this season.

### We Control Our Thinking and Our Speech

If we're going to experience the outpouring of God's of marvels, wonders, and extraordinary manifestations of His greatness, we must be deliberate in removing any self-imposed limitations. Two ways we limit our ability to receive all God has in store for us are by our *small thinking* and our *negative speech*. Small thinking and negative speech go hand in hand; therefore, we need to get rid of them both.

For instance, we must quit saying things such as "That could never happen to me. That only happens to people like Oral Roberts or Billy Graham." Are we children of God? Are we believers? Then we are qualified to receive His marvels, wonders, and extraordinary manifestations.

Some say, "Well, Brother Jerry, I've never been able to think big." If they'd get in the Word more, the Word would enlarge their capacity to think big. We all start out being small thinkers. I wasn't able to think big—as I do now—when I first started my walk of faith. When I was new to the Lord, before I'd ever preached my first sermon, I'd never thought about getting out of Shreveport, much less moving my family to Texas. But now from our headquarters in Crowley, Texas, this ministry has touched the four corners of the earth. I've been in forty-six nations and preached to as few as one and as many as a hundred thousand, and my messages and resources have gone around the world. I couldn't even think big enough to imagine any of these things in the beginning, but spending time with God and being in the presence of other people of faith enlarged my thinking.

One of the aspects I appreciate most about the relationship I had with Oral Roberts is that he taught me how to think big. In fact, he prominently displayed a metal plaque on his desk that read MAKE NO LITTLE PLANS HERE. Many times when he was around someone who exhibited small-minded thinking, Brother Roberts would turn his head away and not look at them.

I remember him turning away from me one time during a conversation. I said, "Brother Roberts, are you listening to me?"

He said, "No."

"Why not?"

"You think too small," he said as he turned his back to me. I had to walk around in front of him to get him to look at me. That's when he said, "When you start thinking bigger, I'll look at you."

That experience was a little embarrassing, but it was also challenging in that it I learned to think bigger. I didn't mind the challenge and correction, because I didn't want to continue to think small and speak negative words. The Bible says, *Rebuke is more effective for a wise man than a hundred blows on a fool* (Proverbs 17:10). I've been rebuked by some of the best, and every reproof enlarged me and enabled me to move to another level.

If we're going to experience marvels, wonders, and

extraordinary manifestations of God's greatness, we have to remove the barriers of small thinking and negative speech. We have to allow our imaginations to soar to new levels. Many people think the human imagination is evil, but it isn't. It's a God-given gift. We have been given the ability to imagine, but it's up to us to use our imagination for God's purposes and not for evil. The Bible speaks of pulling down strongholds in the realm of the mind, saying, *Casting down imaginations, and every high thing [thought] that exalteth itself against the knowledge of God* (2 Corinthians 10:5 KJV). These types of imaginations are the only imaginations we are to cast down.

We are to think on the Word, on things that are just, lovely, and of good report. We can be selective about what we think. We have the ability to use our imagination all the time, so let's use it in a positive way.

Some people get up in the morning and imagine themselves failing that day. They imagine losing their jobs; they can almost see it happening. They can hear the words they imagine their boss will say. If they don't cast down those thoughts, they will eventually begin to speak them: "I just know I won't be at this job much longer." "My boss will probably fire me." They don't realize they are prophesying their own doom. Jesus said, *"For out of the abundance of the heart the mouth speaks"* (Matthew 12:34).

When we were born again, we were recreated as a new spirit being, in line with the nature of God. We now have the Holy Spirit living inside of us, and we have the mind of Christ. We have the ability to imagine what God imagines and think His thoughts. We can live life without the world's limitations—if we are willing to remove the self-imposed barriers of small thinking and negative speech.

Psalms 78 provides a beautiful synopsis of the great things God did for the children of Israel as He led them through the wilderness before entering the Promised Land.

He divided the sea and caused them to pass through; and He made the waters stand up like a heap. In the daytime also He led them with the cloud, and all the night with a light of fire. He split the rocks in the wilderness, and gave them drink in abundance like the depths. He also brought streams out of the rock, and caused waters to run down like rivers.

Behold, He struck the rock, so that the waters gushed out, and the streams overflowed (Psalms 78:13–16, 20).

The children of Israel had already seen all the marvelous things God had done, but every time they had a new challenge, and every time a new adversity arose, they forgot what they'd seen and what God had done: *Yes, they spoke against God: They said, "Can God prepare a table in the wilderness?"* (verse 19). Sadly, people in churches throughout the world today still ask, "Can God really meet this need? Can God *really* do miracles?"

Most of us have experienced miracles in our lives. When something out of the usual happens that cannot be explained by human reason, we don't question that God was the source of it. But then time passes, and we have another need or another challenge. That's when it's easy to forget what God has already done, what He has already shown us. We tend to waver between faith and unbelief, big thinking and small thinking, negative speech and faith-filled speech. That's what happened to the children of Israel: *They did not believe in God, and did not trust in His salvation* (verse 22). Then we read further in Psalms 78 and see this: *Then they remembered that God was their rock, and the Most High God their Redeemer* (verse 35).

Notice God's people were back and forth in their thinking. One moment they didn't remember anything He'd done; the next moment they recalled He was their rock. Their thinking and speech actually limited God from showing His wonders, marvels, and extraordinary manifestations in their behalf: *How often they provoked Him in the wilderness, and grieved Him in the desert! Yes, again and again they tempted God, and limited the Holy One of Israel. They did not remember His power: the day when He redeemed them from the enemy, when He worked His signs in Egypt, and His wonders in the field of Zoan* (Psalms 78:40-43).

The children of Israel limited God through their small thinking and negative talk. That's why it's so important that we learn to do as 2 Corinthians 10:5 says, to bring every thought into captivity to the obedience of Christ, and then boldly declare, "I expect marvels, wonders, and extraordinary manifestations of God's greatness in my life!"

**Big Thinking Brings Big Results**

I could write an entire book detailing the marvels, wonders, and extraordinary manifestations Carolyn and I have experienced, not only in our personal lives, but also in our ministry over the past five decades. As wonderful as these experiences have been, I believe the best is yet to come.

When the Bible talks about God's wonders, it almost always refers to things that are yet to be seen. For instance, when the apostle Paul wrote, *"Eye has not seen, nor ear heard, nor have entered into the heart of man the things which God has prepared for those who love Him"* (1 Corinthians 2:9), he was referring to things that had not yet happened.

In chapter 2 we learned that God is the God of surprises and there is no end to His surprises. I want to challenge you to get up every morning and expect surprises. You might say, "But, Brother Jerry, something isn't a surprise if I'm expecting it." We can expect to be surprised, but it's usually at the way God accomplishes it that surprises us. I don't doubt God is going to meet my every need; I just never know how He is going to do it.

This principle is particularly true when it comes to His financial blessings. One day I got a call from a man who asked me to come to his office. When I arrived, he was leaning back in his chair, his cowboy-booted feet on the desk. He stood up, shook my hand, and then asked his wife to come into the office. I didn't have a clue what he wanted.

His wife joined us, and then he pushed an envelope across the desk to me and said, "I just wanted to see how you would react to what's in this envelope."

I opened the envelope and pulled out a check made out for one million dollars to our ministry. That's when I heard God say, "Surprise!"

I wasn't surprised that I'd just received a check for one million dollars. Over the years our ministry had received numerous combinations of checks totaling a million dollars, but I'd been confessing for a long time to my staff that one day we would receive a single check for one million dollars.

The man saw the big smile that came across my face, and he said, "Are you surprised?"

"No, sir," I said. "I'm not surprised to receive a check in this amount; however, I'm surprised that God used you to give it to our ministry. When I laid my eyes on your check, I heard the Lord say, 'Surprise!' He was referring to how He made it happen and who He used to make it happen."

I'd been thinking big and speaking words of faith that someday our ministry would receive a check for one million dollars. I believed what I'd said; therefore, I wasn't surprised when it happened. The day I received that check, I enlarged my thinking and declared, "This one million dollar check is the first of many!"

Thinking big brings big results.

Jesus taught His disciples the importance of the words we speak, saying, *"Have faith in God. For assuredly, I say to you, whoever says to this mountain, 'Be removed and be cast into the sea,' and does not doubt in his heart, but believes that those things he says will be done, he will have whatever he says"* (Mark 11:22–24). This is why we need to get rid of words produced by small thinking, such as "That can never happen to me" or "Can God *really* do for me what He did for someone else?" We need to quit saying "Can He?" and instead declare "He can!"

In the book of Genesis, we find the account of the promise God made to Abraham and Sarah, who had never had children:

> And He said, "I will certainly return to you according to the time of life, and behold, Sarah your wife shall have a son."
> (Sarah was listening in the tent door which was behind him.) Now Abraham and Sarah were old, well advanced in age; and Sarah had passed the age of childbearing. Therefore Sarah laughed within herself, saying, "After I have grown old, shall I have pleasure, my lord being old also?"
> And the Lord said to Abraham, "Why did Sarah laugh, saying, 'Shall I surely bear a child, since I am old?' I there anything too hard for the Lord? At the appointed time I will return to you, according to the time of life, and Sarah shall have a son" (Genesis 18:10–13).

In the natural, God's promise seemed impossible to Abraham. God understood Abraham's mindset, which is why He helped Abraham enlarge his thinking. Then [God] brought [Abraham] outside and said, "Look now toward heaven, and count the stars if you are able to number them." And He said to him, "So shall your descendants be" (Genesis 15:5).

God didn't expect Abraham to literally number the stars; rather, He encouraged Abraham to think bigger, to use his imagination. This is what He wants us to do as well.

There's nothing wrong with seeing yourself out of debt, and having plenty left over after all the bills are paid. There's nothing wrong with seeing yourself not having to uses your finances to pay notes anymore. There's nothing wrong with seeing yourself as the giver you've always wanted to be, enlarging the amount of your financial gifts and blessing more individuals and ministries. Thinking bigger and using your imagination for God's purposes are good things. Imagine God taking you by the hand one night and stepping into your front yard. Imagine Him saying, "Look to the heavens and tell me how many stars you see; this is how big you should be thinking."

Remember, it was God who initiated the conversation with Abraham, not the other way around. Just as God encouraged Abraham to think bigger and use his imagination, so He wants us to enlarge our thinking and expand our vision so that we can accomplish what He's called us to do.

I remember flying one day with Brother Copeland in the first airplane he'd believed God for. It was a debt-free Cessna Skylane, a single-engine plane. As we flew over the farmland on the north side of Fort Worth, I noticed a runway below us as and thought perhaps we were going to land. Brother Copeland flew low to scatter the cattle that were on the runway, and then he flew back around and did a touch and go, a maneuver in which the aircraft touches the ground momentarily but then takes off again without landing. While the wheels were on the ground, he looked at me and said, "Jerry, I want you to hear me say this: one day I'm going to own this place, and I'll build my headquarters here." And then we took off again.

A few minutes later we did another touch and go, and he said again, "Hear me say this: one day I'm going to own this place, and I'll build my headquarters here." He flew around and performed a third touch and go, and repeated the words he'd said before.

At the time, Brother Copeland didn't have a lot of money; he'd been in the ministry for only a few years. Although he'd used his faith to get his first debt-free airplane, he certainly didn't have the kind of money it would take to buy that place. But he was saying it every time he did a touch and go that day; he was letting his imagination soar. He was speaking to the mountain of impossibility just as Jesus did when He explained, *"Have faith in God. For assuredly, I say to you, whoever says to this mountain, 'Be removed and be cast into the sea,' and does not doubt in his heart, but believes that those things he says will be done, he will have whatever he says"* (Mark 11:23).

At the time Brother Copeland first made these declarations, his ministry occupied a small office space in a tiny building. My office was the hallway to the bathroom. We'd built some shelves on one side of the hallway so that I could duplicate the ministry's reel-to-reel tapes, and if anyone needed to use the bathroom, I'd have to leave. The hall wasn't wide enough for anyone to get past if I was duplicating tapes.

In the natural there was no way Brother Copeland could own all that acreage where he'd done the touch and go maneuvers, and build his headquarters there. But he kept believing and kept sowing seed for that property, and it wasn't too long before we moved into a bigger office. After a few years we moved into another facility twice the size of the previous one. Not only that, he was flying a bigger and better airplane.

Brother Copeland's vision didn't come to pass in a month, a year, or even a few years. After the Lord led me to launch my own ministry, it was a number of years before Brother Copeland's vision came to pass. That farmland property that looked like a mountain of impossibility the day we did those touch and go maneuvers is now the headquarters of Kenneth Copeland Ministries and Eagle Mountain International Church. And just thirty miles south of Brother Copeland's headquarters is another tract of land that is the home of *Jerry Savelle Ministries International*.

Our ministries have worked together for fifty years now as we have sown the seed of the gospel on literally every continent on Earth. While we may be unable to count the exact number of people who have been touched by our ministries, we know, according to the Word of God, our spiritual descendants will be as the stars in the heavens.

Let your imagination soar. Never let go of the vision God has given you, and never stop speaking it!

**Another Level of Faith**

It takes vision to see wonders, marvels, and extraordinary manifestations of God's greatness come to pass in our lives. If we say, "Nothing like that ever happens to me," then it won't. We should never be angry with someone who is operating at a greater level of faith than we are. We should hook up with them, because they'll pull us up to their level of faith. That's what happened when I had the privilege of working for Brother Copeland.

I remember how God once demonstrated this principle of moving to another level to me through the game of golf. I'd never played before, but at the invitation of a man I knew, I went and played with him. I was terrible; I hit my ball first into trees and then into the water. I should have stopped playing after that initial experience, but at the man's insistence, I played with him again. I wasn't any better the second time.

One of my board members was a great golfer, and he asked me to play with him. When I told him about my previous experience and how poorly I'd played, he said, "Well, was the guy you played with any good?"

"Not really, but he was better than me," I said.

"Let me ask you this, Brother Jerry: if you could play with someone who knows what he's doing and can show you what to do, would it take your game to another level?"

I said, "Yes. Let's go play golf!"

I played several times with this man, and each time I was around him, observing how he played and listening to his advice, my game improved. Just being around someone who knew what he was doing took my game to another level.

If you're struggling with your faith, get around people who know what they're doing. Put yourself in a faith environment and learn to operate with a no-limits mentality. Never allow yourself to be frustrated with people who think bigger than you do—that is, if you want to see God's marvels, wonders, and extraordinary manifestations of His greatness.

As we prepare for an outpouring of these things in our lives, we need to enlarge our vision and thinking, and we need to speak in line with God's covenant: *"I am making a covenant with you. Before all your people I will do wonders never before done in any nation in all the world"* (Exodus 34:10 NIV). We need to expect His wonders, those things that are unfamiliar and cannot be explained, things only God can make happen. We need to stand in faith for His marvels, those extraordinary occurrences that arrest our attention and cause us to stand in awe with an overwhelming sense of admiration and reverence for God. And we need to confidently await the remarkable, uncommon, rare, special, and extraordinary manifestations of His greatness.

I want to challenge you to join me in doing three things on a daily basis.

First, think about God's promised wonders, marvels, and manifestations. The Word of God says, *For as [a man] thinks in his heart, so is he* (Proverbs 23:7). What you choose to think about most and what you dwell on most will eventually come to pass in your life. You become what you think about most; your life tends to go in the direction of your most dominant thoughts.

Second, decree that marvels, wonders, and manifestations are taking place in your life. Don't just talk about this occasionally; exercise your faith by making the declaration daily. The

Bible says, *And since we have the same spirit of faith, according to what is written, "I believed and therefore I spoke," we also believe and therefore speak* (2 Corinthians 4:13). If you truly believe something, you're going to talk about it.

Third, expect God's wonders, marvels, and manifestations—every day. To expect something implies a sense of excitement. Think about how excited children become prior to Christmas; they expect the celebration to be wonderful. They get excited at just the thought of what will happen Christmas Day. Well, our God is the wonder-working God; therefore, we should leave it to Him to show us His wonders; our job is to expect them.

The psalmist David said, *My soul, wait thou only upon God; for my expectation is from him. He only is my rock and my salvation: he is my defense; I shall not be moved* (Psalms 62:5–6 KJV). And in the book of Proverbs we read these words: *For surely there is an end; and thine expectation shall not be cut off* (Proverbs 23:18 KJV). The Message translation says, *Then you won't be left with an armload of nothing.* In other words, we act on our faith in God's covenant coming to pass by thinking about it, decreeing it, and expecting it. When we do these things on a consistent basis, we won't be left with an armload of nothing.

Some of the first marvels, wonders, and extraordinary manifestations we will experience may be in the area of financial breakthroughs and restoration. Such manifestations will cause others to stand in admiration and reverence of our God. The Bible speaks of God's time of restoration prior to the coming of Jesus: *And that He may send Jesus Christ, who was preached to you before, whom heaven must receive until the times of restoration of all things, which God has spoken by the mouth of all His holy prophets since the world began* (Acts 3:20–21). One of the great marvels that will take place before the appearing of Jesus will be the restoration of everything Satan has stolen from us.

If you're ready to get back everything the enemy has stolen from you, I encourage you to get up every day and declare, "Today is my blessing day. Today is my receiving day. Today is my restoration day. Today is my day for a surprise. Today is my day for marvels, wonders, and extraordinary manifestations of God's greatness in my life!"

Don't ever give up on God or His Word. Stay in faith and prepare for the outpouring that has been prepared for our generation to receive!

# PART 2
## The Ministry of Angels

*Are they not all ministering spirits sent forth to minister for those who will inherit salvation.*
*— Hebrews 1:14*

# CHAPTER 4
## We Are Heirs of Salvation

For many, our earliest awareness of angels came through hearing the story of the nativity, in which the angel of the Lord spoke to the shepherds, followed by a multitude of angels singing and giving glory to God. Some of us learned at an early age that we each have a guardian angel who continually watches over us. The Scripture clearly supports the existence of angels, yet it's a topic that is not frequently addressed in our churches.

Angels are mentioned almost two hundred times in the Bible; therefore, it's important we have an understanding about these remarkable beings and their role in the affairs of mankind. You may say, "Wait a minute, Brother Jerry, what do angels have to do with what you've been talking about?" The world is changing at a rapid pace, and the body of Christ is functioning in a place it's never known before. In this new season the marvels, wonders, and extraordinary manifestations of God's greatness will come about in part through the ministry of angels.

The first line of Hebrews 2 says, *Therefore we must give the more earnest heed to the things which we have heard, lest at any time we should let them slip* (KJV). To understand what "things" this verse refers to, let's back up to the closing verses of Hebrews 1: *But to which of the angels said he at any time, sit on my right hand, until I make thine enemies thy footstool? Are they not all ministering spirits, sent forth to minister for them who shall be heirs of salvation?* (verses 13–14 KJV).

To whom does God send the angels? To those who are heirs of salvation—that's us! The ministry of angels didn't cease with the announcement of the birth of Jesus and the subsequent hallelujah choir in the heavenlies. Angels are mentioned 175 times in the New Testament, 21 times alone in the book of Acts.

My wife often tells others that her encounters with angels began when she was only eight years old, after she'd been filled with the Holy Ghost one night at her church's youth camp. Carolyn was there with her sister, and when their parents came to pick them up for the forty-mile drive home, Carolyn was unable speak a word in English. She was so overwhelmed by the presence of the Holy Ghost that she prayed in tongues all the way home. As she prayed, she saw angels dancing on the hood of her father's truck throughout the entire drive. Carolyn has experienced the ministry of angels consistently since then.

I wasn't aware of it at the time, but I experienced the ministry of angels before I was born again. Their ministry is the reason I'm still alive. I'm convinced that when I finally surrendered my life to the Lord, my guardian angel rejoiced as he thought, *I kept Jerry alive so he could get saved!*

Again, the Bible says that we are to give earnest heed to the fact that angels are ministering spirits sent in our behalf and we are not to let this fact slip away. But this is exactly what has happened in the Church world today; people don't talk about angels much anymore, and those who do are often considered "flaky." As with any biblical teaching, we should always stay in line with what the Bible actually teaches and not become so focused on one issue that we become spiritually out of balance.

Lester Sumrall was a powerful man of God known for his revelation and Bible-based teaching about demons. Demons are real, and we need to have an understanding of how they operate, but they should never be our focus. I traveled with Brother Sumrall a number of times, and anytime he concluded a teaching session with a period of questions and answers, the first thing people asked about was demons. Brother Sumrall once said, "I have to be careful in talking about demons so that people don't become 'demon chasers.' Those are folks who look for demons everywhere." This is why it's important that we stick with what the Bible says about any topic.

I personally believe the activity of angels, or ministering spirits, is increasing in our day and will continue to do so. I'm convinced many believers have experienced the ministry of angels without knowing it, for the Bible says, *Be not forgetful to entertain strangers: for thereby some have entertained angels unawares* (Hebrews 13:2 KJV).

If we are going to see the marvels, wonders, and extraordinary manifestations of the greatness of God in our lives, then let's not let this revelation about angels slip. They are on assignment and have significant involvement in God's prophetic words coming to pass in these last days.

### The Bible Perspective on Angels

The Word of God says, *Praise Him, all His angels; praise Him, all His hosts! Let them praise the name of the Lord, for He commanded and they were created* (Psalms 148:2, 5). In this verse we see that the words angels and hosts mean the same thing. When the Bible refers to God as the Lord of hosts, it means He is the Lord of angels.

We learn two important facts about angels from these verses. One, angels are never to stop praising God. In Revelation 4:8, we see angels surrounding the throne of God, crying, *"Holy, holy, holy is the Lord God Almighty!"* (NIV). They have been decreeing God's holiness forever and will continue to do so forever. Not once have I read my Bible and found that God said, "Enough is enough. Will someone please tell those angels to stop?" No! He's the one who gave them the assignment to praise Him; He welcomes their praise. Angels don't magnify themselves; they always magnify God.

The second fact we learn from these verses in Psalms 148 is that angels are created beings. God commanded, and the angels were created. If God created the angels, then they have a purpose; that purpose is to minister to the heirs of salvation. The word *angel* in both Hebrew and Greek means "messenger; sent one." Angels are spirit beings that operate primarily in the unseen realm. However, angels can become visible at God's direction, as we see in the following account of Elisha's ministry:

> And the man of God sent unto the king of Israel, saying, Beware that thou pass not such a place; for thither the Syrians are come down.
>
> And the king of Israel sent to the place which the man of God told him and warned him of, and saved himself there, not once or twice.
>
> Therefore sent he thither horses, and chariots, and a great host: and they came by night, and compassed the city about.
>
> And when the servant of the man of God was risen early, and gone forth, behold an host compassed the city both with horses and chariots. And his servant said unto him, Alas, my master! How shall we do?
>
> And he answered, Fear not: for they that be with us are more than they that be with them.
>
> And Elisha prayed, and said, Lord, I pray thee, open his eyes, that he may see. And the Lord opened the eyes of the young man; and he saw: and, behold, the mountain was full of horses and chariots of fire round about Elisha
> (2 Kings 6:9–10, 14–17 KJV).

After Elisha's servant came back with a report that they were surrounded and outnumbered, Elisha sent the young man to look again. When Elisha told the young man there were more with them than there were with the enemy, Elisha was seeing something his servant couldn't see. That's why Elisha asked the Lord to open his servant's eyes. The Message translation says, *The eyes of the young man were opened and he saw. A wonder!*

This story affirms the connection between the ministry of angels and the ministry of marvels, wonders, and extraordinary manifestations of God's greatness. When God opened the eyes of Elisha's servant, he saw what Elisha meant when he'd said, "Fear not, for those who are with us are more than those who are with them."

From this story we see two characteristics of angels: First, they establish a sense of security in the people to whom they are sent. Second, their appearance reveals their might and strength.

Another characteristic of angels is their ability to communicate, as in the ensuing story from the book of Acts. The apostle Paul and others were on a voyage to Rome when Paul issued a warning:

> "Men, I perceive that this voyage will end with disaster and much loss, not only of the cargo and ship, but also our lives." Nevertheless the centurion was more persuaded by the helmsman and the owner of the ship than by the things spoken by Paul.
>
> When the south wind blew softly, supposing that they had obtained their desire, putting out to sea, they sailed close by Crete. But not long after, a tempestuous head wind arose, called Euroclydon.... And because we were exceedingly tempest-tossed, the next day they lightened the ship. On the third day we threw the ship's tackle overboard with our own hands. Now when neither the sun nor stars appeared for many days, and no small tempest beat on us, all hope that we would be saved was finally given up.
>
> But after long abstinence from food, then Paul stood in the midst of them and said, "Men, you should have listened

to me, and not have sailed from Crete and incurred this disaster and loss. And now I urge you to take heart, for there will be no loss of life among you, but only the ship. For there stood by me this night an angel of God to whom I belong and serve, saying, 'Do not be afraid, Paul; you must be brought before Caesar; and indeed God has granted you all those who sail with you.' Therefore take heart, men, for I believe God that it will be just as it was told me" (Acts 27:10–11, 13–25).

When was the last time you heard someone in the path of a hurricane-proportion storm sound this positive and confident? Paul's initial concern for the loss of lives must have departed the moment the angel appeared to Paul and delivered the message from God. Certainly the angel's message brought assurance and gave Paul the confidence everything was going to be okay. Apparently the message encouraged all those aboard, for verse 36 says, *Then were they all of good cheer* (KJV).

The people on that ship with Paul likely knew nothing about God. But because the angel had spoken to Paul (who was in the ship with them as it broke apart and supplies were thrown overboard) and the people saw how he had responded to the message with joy, it cheered them up.

As it turned out, they all escaped safely to land just as the angel said they would. A great miracle of deliverance, a marvel and a wonder, occurred to demonstrate the greatness of God. Only God could have saved them and delivered them.

It was not uncommon in Bible days for God to use angels to manifest marvels, signs, and wonders; therefore, it should not be uncommon for Him to do so today. God is still engaging angels in our behalf though we may not be aware of their presence.

Again, the Bible says, *Be not forgetful to entertain strangers: for thereby some have entertained angels unawares* (Hebrews 13:2 KJV).

I believe we are about to experience a significant increase in testimonies about angels as we enter the days ahead. Angels are far more involved in fulfilling God's will and His plans for our lives than most of us know. The ministry of angels hasn't ceased; it's still in operation today. Supernatural manifestations of angels are becoming more prominent as we move closer to the appearing of the Lord.

It's important to understand that angels don't appear because we ask or tell them to; they appear when it is God's will they do so. However, we can and should expect their involvement in our lives. The Bible says angels are sent forth to minister to those who will inherit salvation (see Hebrews 1:14). The word *minister* means "to attend to; to serve; to perform service for." The Message translation says, *"All angels are sent to help out."*

When we understand that God is the one who sends angels to minister in our behalf, we can move confidently through life, knowing we will have the help we need to face any encounter or situation.

## My Encounters with Angels

Before I share a few of my own encounters with angels that occurred prior to my salvation, it's important that you understand my spiritual condition at the time.

Prior to surrendering my life to the Lord, I'd been on the run from God since something significant occurred when I was ten years old. That was in 1957, and I was with my parents and other family members at my grandmother's home on Thanksgiving Day in Oklahoma City. Someone had turned on the old black-and-white television set so that the adults could watch Oral Roberts. I'd never heard of the man, but while I stood there holding my plate of food, I was captivated as I watched him pray for the sick and then saw the miracles that followed. That's when I heard a voice say, "Someday you will preach like that; someday you will pray for sick people like that."

At first I thought one of my cousins, Joe or Donnie, who were standing beside me had spoken. But when I turned around, neither one was there; they'd left the room. That's when I knew the voice I'd just heard hadn't been audible—but it had been the voice of God. But I didn't want to acknowledge it—and especially didn't want to give heed to what He had said.

By age ten I'd already planned my life, and I knew exactly what I was going to do. My dad was in the automotive business; he repaired wrecked vehicles, restored classic automobiles, built hot rods, and raced cars. I wanted him to teach me everything he knew so that I could spend the rest of my life doing the same thing. I'd already made up my mind that I was going to own my own business and do everything my dad had done. This preaching business would ruin my plans, so I never told anyone about what I'd heard. In my young mind I reasoned that if I ever told anyone about it, then I'd have to do it.

My best friend at the time was a boy named Kenny who lived across the street from me. At the end of our street was a little Baptist church where our parents took us each Sunday. Kenny and I always got together at church, and if our parents allowed it, we would sit together. The problem was that Kenny and I would get to talking while the preacher was preaching and then we'd have to go sit with our parents.

One day we were sitting together in church quietly for a change. When the preacher gave the invitation for salvation at the end of the message, I watched as Kenny got up and walked down to the front of the sanctuary and got saved. I was shocked.

When Kenny returned to his seat beside me, I said, "Why didn't you tell me you were going to do that?"

He looked at me and said, "I didn't know I was going to do it."

I thought, *Well then, I'll do it next Sunday.* And that's just what

I did. I didn't have a clue about what I was doing, and I don't remember the preacher asking me if I believed Jesus was the Son of God or if I wanted Him to save me. He just gave me a card to fill out and said, "We'll baptize you in water tonight." After I got baptized in water, they told me I was saved, but I didn't feel any different. All I felt was wet.

So according to the church down the street, Kenny and I were both saved. As far as I was concerned, nothing was different. I didn't get a Bible and began to study salvation or anything else. It wasn't long before I simply ignored the experience and at some point stopped going to church for a while. But as time passed, anytime I was in a church or anyplace where the presence of God was, I had to get out quick. I couldn't have identified the feeling at the time, but I now understand that I was under conviction. I knew if I stayed long enough for God to speak to me again, then I'd have to preach. And I wasn't going to preach!

I went on with my plans for my life, learning from my dad and working on cars with him as I grew into young adulthood. I was earning money doing paint and body work but then a friend told me that the army ammunition plant about twenty-five miles from where we lived was hiring people to work on the weekend. I could use the extra money, so I applied for the job and got it.

My assignment was to work on a lathe to help make the motor shells the plant was responsible for supplying to the army. One weekend my foreman stopped and said they needed some volunteers to find out why the huge pipes that carried the flushed-out shavings were backed up. He offered double pay for the rest of the weekend, so I volunteered.

To get to the area of the backup, I had to go through a manhole and then down a set of steps that went to the area beneath the plant. When I reached the bottom, I was standing in water up to my knees, but it was dark and I couldn't see well enough to determine the source of the problem. I shouted for someone to bring in a light and hold it above me so that I could see. A few minutes later a light appeared at the end of an extension cord. But to my horror, I looked up at the exact moment that someone dropped the light. I realized the instant it made contact with the water, I would be electrocuted.

I remember thinking, *I don't want to die,* and then watching as the light went out a split second before hitting the water. I climbed out of that hole and said, "I don't care what you're paying. I'm not going back down there!"

It was then I discovered they'd carelessly plugged the extension cord into an exterior sidewall and someone had walked by and tripped on the cord. The cord had come unplugged only a fraction of a second before hitting the water and electrocuting me. The thought never left me at how "lucky" I'd been that day.

I managed to stay out of church as much as possible until I met and married Carolyn, who went to a different kind of church. It was a Pentecostal church, and I'd never seen anything like it in my life. Oftentimes the presence of God was so heavy in the place that I'd get up and leave. When Carolyn would ask where I was going, I'd just tell her I had to get out. When she asked why I had to get out, I couldn't tell her it was because at age ten God had called me to preach; I certainly wasn't going to give her any leverage to use against me.

Carolyn knew in her heart I was called to preach, and she knew I was running from God. But I was also perfectly happy to be working in my own business. My Dad and I built racecars and hauled them all over the southeastern part of the United States. I restored classic cars, worked on hot rods, and did paint and body work. My dad was so proud of me because he'd always wanted to go into business for himself but had never made the leap. I loved what I did and could hardly wait to go to work each morning.

I was still running from God and going to church only occasionally which was the source of regular arguments between Carolyn and me. I remember being so angry one night at her telling me that I needed to go to church that I went out and got into my 1965 GTO and burned rubber all the way down the street when I left our little house. A railroad track crossed our street a short distance away, and I was doing close to 100 mph when my car jumped the track. I heard a loud noise behind me at the same time I felt the impact of a powerful wind against the car. When I looked in my rear view mirror, I saw the speeding train that had missed hitting me by literally a fraction of a second. I was so scared that I stopped the car, got out, sat down on the side of the road, and just shook.

Another time I was working on my '57 Chevrolet that I drag raced. My dad had always told me, "Son, don't ever get under that car without putting stands under it first." I knew what I needed to do to ensure my safety, but I was in a hurry to get the car ready to go. I'd put the floor jack under the car so that I could remove the rear wheels, but I didn't put the stands under it. I took the wheels off and then got under the car—just as the jack collapsed. All I saw was the car coming down, and I knew that, with no wheels to break the fall, the frame would crush me.

The next thing I knew, I was no longer beneath the car; I was sitting on the ground looking at my Chevy. I had no idea how I'd gotten there, but I knew it was humanly impossible to have moved from beneath that car so quickly. I was so scared that I shook just as badly as I had when that train missed my GTO by less than a split second. That experience almost convinced me to go to church—but not quite.

At the time of each of these incidents, I didn't realize angels had intervened to save my life. After I surrendered my life to the Lord and He began to teach me about angels, He said, "Son, you've encountered angels all your life. You just didn't know it. Think about the time you were almost electrocuted, the time you crossed the railroad track doing about 100 mph, and the time the car fell but you escaped. Each time I sent an angel to protect you."

I believe in angels, and I believe they are assigned to work in behalf of those who are heirs of salvation. But I also believe that, according to the Word of God, one of their assignments is to keep us alive. You may think that once I turned my life over to God, my need for angelic protection ceased. But that was not the case. In fact, as I continue sharing my encounters with angels, you'll see I needed their protection more than ever.

# CHAPTER 5
## Angels on Assignment

One of the world's most widely recognized works of art is Michelangelo's *Creation of Adam*, which forms part of the Sistine Chapel's ceiling. The iconic image of the almost-touching hands of God and Adam is one of the most replicated paintings of all time.

God is depicted in this painting as an elderly white-bearded man wrapped in a swirling cloak and surrounded by twelve human-like figures, several of which are portrayed as chubby children. Although the identity of these twelve beings is unclear, it's possible Michelangelo's chubby children served as inspiration for other artists who sought to personify angels in their creative works.

In reality, angels are not the fat, little naked characters wielding bows and arrows that artists have portrayed them to be. We don't find any such description of angels in the Bible. Can you image the angels Michael or Gabriel appearing in such a form? No! When Gabriel showed up, his appearance struck fear in the hearts of those who saw him.

The prophet Daniel said this about Gabriel: *So he came near me where I stood, and when he came I was afraid and fell on my face* (Daniel 8:17). Gabriel was sent to the elderly priest Zacharias to announce the birth of John. The Bible says, *Then an angel of the Lord appeared to [Zacharias], standing on the right side of the altar of incense. And when Zacharias saw him, he was troubled, and fear fell upon him* (Luke 1:11–12).

Jude identifies Michael as the archangel who contended with the devil about the body of Moses. In the book of Revelation, we see Michael and his angels at war with the devil and his angels, who are ultimately cast out. God's angels are not the little, fat characters we see on Valentine's Day cards; angels are mighty created beings whose purpose is to minister in behalf of the heirs of salvation—that's us!

The ninety-first psalm is a powerful verbal depiction of God's protection for those who choose to put their trust in Him.

> He who dwells in the secret place of the Most High shall abide under the shadow of the Almighty. I will say of the Lord, "He is my refuge and my fortress; My God, in Him I will trust."
>
> Because you have made the Lord, who is my refuge, even the Most High, your dwelling place, no evil shall befall you, nor shall any plague come near your dwelling; for He shall give His angels charge over you, to keep you in all your ways. In their hands they shall bear you up, lest you dash your foot against a stone (Psalms 91:1–2, 9–12).

Notice this passage says that God will give His angels charge over us. The original Hebrew word translated as charge means to "enjoin; appoint; send with; send a messenger; set in order." In other words, God's angels are appointed and sent with us as both messengers and purveyors of order and protection.

So angels have been given assignments from God to work with us and for us. The Bible says, *Bless the Lord, you His angels, who excel in strength, who do His word, heeding the voice of His word* (Psalms 103:20). The Message translation says, *So bless God, you angels, ready and able to do what he says ... alert to respond to whatever he wills.* This is good news!

In the previous chapter I shared some of my experiences with angels before I got saved and was aware that angels were involved in my life. I've continued to experience angelic visitations throughout my life and ministry.

I recall one weekend in the early 1970s when Carolyn, our girls, and I were driving to Shreveport from Fort Worth where we had planned to visit family. At that time the turnpike between the two cities was the best way to travel, so that's the road we took. But as we got on the turnpike that day, rain started coming down so hard that the windshield wipers were of little use. The turnpike had four lanes on each side, and our vehicle was in one of the two center eastbound lanes. With traffic on either side as well as in front and back of our vehicle, it probably wasn't safe to drive more than 30 mph.

Ahead of me in the lane next to mine was a huge truck with a trailer that was swerving on the slick road. I wanted to move to another lane and put some distance between my vehicle and the trailer, but there was too much traffic, and I couldn't move. I glanced at my speedometer and noted the traffic was moving at about 40 mph, and when I looked back up, I saw the truck driver losing control of his truck and trailer as it slid into the lane right in front of me.

I knew if I hit my brakes, I'd go into a slide and the cars behind me would pile into us. There was absolutely no way to avoid hitting that rig broadside—with my wife and children in the car with me. That's when I heard Carolyn shout, "Jesus, help us!"

The next thing I knew, our vehicle was ahead of the traffic; the truck and trailer was behind us, rolled over in the ditch where it had slid off the turnpike. I don't have a clue how that incident happened in the natural; I just know it happened. When Carolyn and I told her parents, about our experience, they said matter-of-factly, "Oh, that was an angel. We've had things like that happen many times in our lives."

Another time I was traveling south on Interstate 35 at about one in the morning with Carolyn and the girls asleep in the car. We'd been to my grandmother's funeral in Oklahoma City and were on our way back to Fort Worth. Ordinarily we wouldn't have been on the road that late, but I didn't get to see my Oklahoma cousins very often so we'd stayed and visited with them until around midnight.

I was reflecting on the day and enjoying the peace of a traffic-free road ahead when I felt a bump and heard a noise so loud it woke everyone up. Carolyn said, "What was that?" I told her I'd hit something in the road but everything was okay; she and the girls could go back to sleep. As my family slept, I continued the drive south; however, at some point I looked at my fuel gage and saw the needle rapidly moving toward the empty mark. Whatever I'd run over had obviously knocked a hole in my fuel tank.

I pulled the car to the side of the road and took my flashlight from the glove compartment. When I looked under the car, I saw gasoline drizzling steadily from the fuel tank. By then it was after two in the morning, and we were stranded on a highway in the Oklahoma boondocks. I didn't know how far it was to the next town, and I couldn't recall how far back the last town we'd passed had been. We didn't have cell phones back then, and I didn't want to take off walking to find help and leave my family alone in the car. I said, "Carolyn, we have to pray that God will send us some help," and that's just what we did.

*We joined hands and prayed, and then because Jesus said, "Therefore I say to you, whatever things you ask when you pray, believe that you receive them, and you will have them"* (Mark 24), we thanked God for sending someone. We sat there for some time, continuing to thank God as we prayed in the Spirit, and then I noticed distant headlights appear in my rear view mirror.

"Carolyn, someone is coming," I said as I picked up my flashlight. I got out of my car and started waving the flashlight until a white truck pulled up behind my car. When a man got out and walked toward me I said, "Can you help me?"

He said, "That's what I was sent for."

I didn't think about his odd response as I went on to explain, "I ran over something in the highway, and it knocked a hole in my gas tank. Now I've lost all my fuel."

"No problem," he said as he went and got a chain from his truck. He pulled his vehicle in front of mine and used the chain to hook the front of my car to the back of his truck. When I asked how far it was to the next town, he said, "About twenty miles. I'll tow you to the exit, and then we're going to cross over the highway. There's a gas station on the left-hand side."

The man towed us to the next exit, and sure enough, there was a little station on the left side of the highway. It was a small, two-pump station that appeared to have been built in the 1940s. Right next to it was a little old café—both were closed. I didn't know what good a closed station would do me in the middle of the night, but the truck driver pulled to a stop, got out of his truck, and took a set of keys out of his pocket. He unlocked the door to the service station, turned on the lights, and then went and raised the door to the bay area.

We pushed my car inside, and then he went to work on it. After he plugged my gas tank, we pushed the car back outside, and he filled the tank with gas. Then he turned and said, "I think that will do it."

I said, "Sir, you don't know what this means to me. You were a blessing to me and to my family. I don't know what we would have done if you hadn't showed up."

Again he said, "That's what I was sent for."

I thanked the man and tried to pay him, but he wouldn't accept my money. When I asked to at least pay for the fuel, all he said was, "That's what I was sent for."

Carolyn and I drove the rest of the way back to Fort Worth praising God and rejoicing at the way He'd sent help and rescued us.

About six weeks later as I was getting ready to go back to Oklahoma City for a meeting, I told Carolyn that, on the way there, I was going to stop at that service station and thank that man again for what he'd done for us. As I drove north I was watching for the little station and the café, but by the time I spotted them, I'd already missed the exit, so I had to go to the next exit and come back. When I pulled into the station, I was surprised to see it was closed and locked up; it looked as if nobody had been there for years.

The café next door was open, so I went inside and asked the owner if he knew the man who owned the station next door. He said, "Son, that service station has been closed for years."

"No, it hasn't," I said. "I had an accident one night on the highway about six weeks ago, and a man towed my car to that station and repaired my gas tank."

"It didn't happen here, son," he said. "That place has been closed for years. Besides, there's no electricity."

I insisted, "I'm telling you, he repaired my tank and then filled it with gas from one of those pumps."

"That's impossible. Those tanks have been dry for years, the place doesn't have electricity. It couldn't have happened at that station."

I walked outside and looked at the station again. "Lord," I said, "isn't this where that happened?"

"It is," He said.

On my way to Oklahoma City, I pondered my conversation with the café owner and what God had said to me when I asked Him about it. Finally I said, "Lord, please explain this to me."

"Son, do you remember what the man kept saying to you the night he came and repaired your car?"

"Yes. He said, 'That's what I was sent for.' No matter what I said to him, all he would say was, 'That's what I was sent for.'"

That's when the Lord said to me, "Son, you entertained an angel."

Those words from the Lord opened my eyes and revealed the event that had occurred six week earlier as a marvel, a wonder, and an extraordinary manifestation of the greatness of God. He demonstrated to me that angels play a significant role in the lives of believers today, just as they did in Bible days.

When Daniel was cast into the den of lions, the king spoke to him, saying, *"Your God, whom you serve continually, He will deliver you"* (Daniel 6:16). When the king arose the next morning to see if Daniel's God had indeed delivered him, Daniel said, *"O king, live forever! My God sent His angel and shut the lions' mouths, so that they have not hurt me"* (verses 21–22).

Daniel came out of the lions' den without a scratch. It was a marvel, a wonder, and an extraordinary manifestation of the greatness of God that was witnessed by all. Notice it was not God alone involved in this miracle: He sent an angel.

The Lord keeps saying to me, "Son, My people are headed for marvels, wonders, and extraordinary manifestations of My greatness such as the world has never seen." Jesus spoke of the end times, saying, *"For nation will rise against nation, and kingdom against kingdom. And there will be famines, pestilences, and earthquakes in various places"* (Matthew 24:8). And yet He said, *"See that you are not troubled"* (verse 6). Could it be that one of the reasons we should not be troubled is that God's angels are charged to be with us and protect us?

### Protection for Us and for Our Children

I love motorcycles and have been riding them all of my life. One of the outreaches of my ministry is the *Chariots of Light Christian Bikers,* a group of enthusiasts who love to ride and share the gospel while doing so (see www.chariotsoflight.org).

Prior to the inception of Chariots of Light when I had a short period of time without any scheduled meetings, I decided to take a couple of days to ride my motorcycle, enjoy the sunshine, and have a good time. When Carolyn asked where I planned to go, I said, "I think I'll ride down to San Antonio and have dinner with some of our friends. I'll spend the night there and then be back tomorrow." Carolyn said okay, so I got on my bike and headed south.

Instead of taking the highway, I decided to take the back roads because they were more fun. I was riding a motorcycle that someone had given to me only two weeks earlier; it was a beautiful bike. The view from the winding country road I traveled was stunning, with lots of rolling Texas hills and miles of ranch land. After a while I glanced in my rearview mirror and noticed and old Ford van steadily approaching. After a few minutes it whipped into the next lane to pass me, but instead of passing it pulled alongside me.

Immediately the side door opened, and I saw four outlaw bikers inside—wild looking characters—and they were looking at my bike. One of them held on to the door and reached toward me as the driver edged closer to my bike. I realized their intent was to kick or shove me so that I would run the bike into the ditch, where they would grab it and put it into the van. No telling what they planned to do to me, so I started praying in the Spirit.

When the guy hanging out the door raised his foot to kick my bike, all of a sudden his eyes got big and his mouth fell wide open. I'll never forget the look of fear on his face. Instead of kicking my bike, he slammed the door shut, and the van sped off.

I don't know what that biker saw, but I almost felt a little bit bad for him.

I asked the Lord what had just happened, and He said, "Son, there is an angel on the back of your bike who is a whole lot bigger and badder than those bikers. I opened their eyes to see him, and that's when they took off."

My angel isn't a fat little cherub holding a bow and arrow; he's big, and he's intimidating. I haven't ever actually seen my angel, but others have.

I was in a meeting in Hot Springs, Arkansas, on Main Street where a lot of street people hung out at that time. As I was preaching, a drunk stumbled in, staggered down the aisle, and then lay down on a couple of chairs and went to sleep. I told the people to just ignore him and let him sleep. I continued to preach as he slept, and every once in a while, he would snore.

After a while he opened his eyes and sat up so that he could change his position. When he looked at me, his eyes opened wide and he said, "Brother, what's that behind you?"

I turned to look and didn't see anything, so I told him that nothing was there.

He said, "No, he's tall—and big."

I didn't have a clue what the guy was talking about, but then someone else said, "I see him too!" That's when the Lord let me know they were seeing my angel.

Later that evening the drunk man sobered up enough to tell me that I would walk around a little bit, make a statement, and then stop. He said that when I hesitated, the big man would whisper something in my ear and then I'd preach like I was on fire.

The Bible says, The angel of the Lord encamps all around those who fear Him, and delivers them (Psalms 34:7). I once experienced this truth at a meeting in Pasadena, California. As I was preaching, a man jumped out of his seat and started running toward me, cussing me at the top of his voice. He looked like a wild animal as everyone watched him leap toward the platform; however, instead of landing in front of me, it appeared as if he hit a glass wall and just slid to the floor.

I removed my microphone, got down where he was, and cast the devil out of him. When he came to himself, he didn't even know what he'd done, but everyone there had witnessed the circle of protection God had placed around me.

Not only do the angels protect Carolyn and me, they also protect our children and grandchildren. A number of years ago, our eldest daughter, Jerriann, and her family lived in the Denver area. Their house was high on the side of a mountain, where winters were oftentimes severe. Jerriann had never lived in that climate, so she wasn't used to driving in the kind of snow that had fallen during the night.

As Jerriann was pulling out of their steep driveway to take the main road out of their community and then down the mountain and on to the highway, Carolyn was at our home in Texas praying. She hadn't talked to Jerriann for a couple of days, but she suddenly felt impressed to intercede for her. While Carolyn prayed in the Spirit, the Lord gave her a vision of Jerriann driving down her driveway, unable to stop her car as it headed toward a drop from the side of the mountain. Carolyn cried out, "God, help! Protect my family. Protect my family!"

A short time later Jerriann called Carolyn and said, "Mom, we just had a miracle! I was driving down …"

Carolyn interrupted her and said, "I saw it. I saw what you were doing."

"Mom, I was driving down our driveway and there was ice at the bottom and I couldn't stop the car. When I put my foot on the brake, the car kept sliding. I was looking down in the valley from the mountain, knowing we were going to slide off."

Jerriann told Carolyn that our grandson Mark James, who was about eight years old at the time and seated beside her in the front seat, screamed, "Jesus—help us!" This was at the same time Carolyn was interceding for them.

Jerriann said, "Mom, I can't explain it, but the next thing I knew the car had turned and we were headed down the road to the main exit from our community. When we got to the exit, I stopped the car, and we all praised God, because what had just happened was not humanly possible.

God's promises are sure, and He is faithful to His Word. When God says, *No evil shall befall you, nor shall any plague come near your dwelling; for He shall give His angels charge over you, to keep you in all your ways. In their hands they shall bear you up, lest you dash your foot against a stone* (Psalms 91:10–12), we have the confidence that comes from knowing we are secure in His love and protection.

## Angels Fulfill God's Word

Not only are angels engaged in the lives of God's people, they also play a role in future events as they help bring to pass God's prophetic declarations. God spoke through the prophet Joel, saying, *"And I will show wonders in the heavens and the earth"* (Joel 2:30). Most of the time when we see wonders mentioned in the Bible, angels are involved. One Bible commentary describes wonders as "extraordinary phenomena arresting the attention."

On the day of Pentecost, we began to see the fulfillment of God's prophetic word spoken through Joel. As the people of Jerusalem marveled at the sound of a rushing, mighty wind from heaven, tongues of fire, and believers who were speaking in other languages of the wonderful works of God, Peter said, *"But this is what was spoken by the prophet Joel"* (Acts 2:16). Shortly after Peter spoke these words, believers began to experience angelic visitations.

> Then the high priest rose up, and all those who were with him (which is the sect of the Sadducees), and they were filled with indignation, and laid their hands on the apostles and put them in the common prison. But at night an angel of the Lord opened the prison doors and brought them out, and said, "Go, stand in the temple and speak to the people all the words of this life" (Acts 5:17-20).

An angel of the Lord opened those doors and brought them out, just as the Word of God says in Psalms 91:11: *He shall give His angels charge over you.* Remember, the word *charge* is defined as to "send with" and to "set things right."

The book of Acts is where we find the story about Philip ministering to the Ethiopian eunuch. This event began with a message from an angel: *Now an angel of the Lord spoke to Philip, saying, "Arise and go toward the south along the road which goes down from Jerusalem to Gaza"* (Acts 10:26).

The evangelistic encounter between Cornelius and Peter began with an angelic visitation:

> There was a certain man in Caesarea called Cornelius, a centurion of what was called the Italian Regiment, a devout man and one who feared God with all his household, who gave alms generously to people, and prayed to God always. About the ninth hour of the day he saw clearly in a vision an angel of God coming in and saying to him, "Cornelius!"
>
> And when he observed him, he was afraid, and said, "What it is, lord?"
>
> So he said to him, "Your prayers and your alms have come up for a memorial before God. Now send men to Joppa, and send for Simon whose surname is Peter. He is lodging with Simon, a tanner, whose house is by the sea. He will tell you what you must do." And when the angel who spoke to him had departed, Cornelius called two of his household servants and a devout soldier from among those who waited on him continually. So when he had explained all these things to them, he sent them to Joppa (Acts 10:1–8).

The next day as Peter was praying on the housetop, he had a vision from God. The Bible says, *While Peter thought about the vision, the Spirit said to him, "Behold, three men are seeking you. Arise therefore, go down and go with them, doubting nothing; for I have sent them"* (Acts 10:19–20). Thus began the introduction of the gospel to the Gentiles, and it started with an angelic visitation.

Just as angels played an integral part in the birth of the early Church, so they will play a significant role in the Second Coming of the Lord Jesus Christ. I believe we will see angelic activity increase tremendously as God's prophetic words come to pass in this day in which we live.

You may say, "But, Brother Jerry, I'm not called to the ministry in the same way you are or the apostles of the Bible were; how can I expect to see the ministry of angels in my life?" You can expect to see them ministering in your life and in the life of your family because God has given them charge over you to keep you in all your ways. You don't have to be a preacher to experience this.

When our girls were young, every morning before they left for school, Carolyn would lay her hands on them and pray that the angels would protect them. God honored her prayers because there were times when Jerriann or Terri could have been injured in an accident, had He not intervened in their behalf. Carolyn and I are grandparents now, yet we continue to pray for our family on a regular basis. I invite you to join me now in this prayer of protection your families:

> Father, in the name of Jesus we ask You to dispatch the angels that have been sent to minister, assist, and protect those who are heirs of salvation. Your Word says children are sanctified by believing parents; therefore, we have the right to ask You for divine protection for our children.
>
> Satan has no legal right to touch the lives of our children. We take authority over him and break his power in the name of Jesus. We expect deliverance to come to any of our children who may be bound by the enemy. We expect it to come about through manifestations of Your greatness so that people will marvel at Your love for us.
>
> We believe the angels are dispatched now in the lives of our families; we receive their protection now, and we thank You for it in the name of Jesus. Amen.

# CHAPTER 6
## Angels in Our Financial Harvest

As Jesus spoke to His disciples about the signs of the times and the end of the age, He made this bold statement: *"And the gospel of the kingdom will be preached in all the world as a witness to all the nations, and then the end will come"* (Matthew 24:14). Jesus spoke these words at a time when people traveled either on foot or with the assistance of an animal. It was simply not possible then for the gospel to be preached in all the world; therefore, we can imagine how astounding the Lord's words sounded to those who heard them.

Fast forward to the twenty-first century: We now know planet Earth is round, with a circumference of approximately twenty-four thousand miles. If an F-86 Sabre jet had an unlimited fuel supply, it could fly around the world in about thirty-six hours. And if we weren't required to be in a physical location for a particular meeting, today's technology would allow us to meet online with individuals living in most any country of the world. Unlike those who were part of the early Church, we live in a time when it is *absolutely possible* to preach the gospel in all the world.

Jesus went on to talk about the end-time harvest of souls and the involvement of angels in the process:

> "He who sows the good seed is the Son of Man. The field is the world, the good seeds are the sons of the kingdom, but the tares are the sons of the wicked one. The enemy who sowed them is the devil, the harvest is the end of the age, and

the reapers are the angels. The Son of Man will send out His angels, and they will gather out of His kingdom ... Then the righteous will shine forth as the sun in the kingdom of their Father" (Matthew 13:37–39, 41, 43).

I have been preaching the gospel since 1969. *Jerry Savelle Ministries International* is one of many great ministries and organizations through whom the Lord's mandate to preach the gospel to all the world is being fulfilled. But there is still much work to be done. Jesus said, *"The harvest truly is great, but the laborers are few; therefore pray the Lord of the harvest to send out laborers into His harvest"* (Luke 10:2).

When Jesus sent out the seventy He had selected to go before Him into the cities, He instructed them not to take their own provision, saying, *"And remain in the same house, eating and drinking such as they give, for the laborer is worthy of his wages"* (verse 7). With this statement Jesus established God's method for funding the laborers sent into the harvest: the funding would come through the hands of others. God's funding method has not changed as we approach the end-time harvest of souls; however, Jesus pointed out one significant difference between the early Church's harvest and the end-time harvest. That is, the angels will be involved in the latter process.

Let's look again at Psalms 103: *Bless the Lord, you His angels, who excel in strength, who do His word, heeding the voice of His word. Bless the Lord, all you His hosts, you ministers of His, who do His pleasure* (verses 20–21). We see a command in place for angels to bless the Lord, to praise Him. Remember, the words *angels* and *hosts* are interchangeable; these amazing beings excel in strength as they minister according to God's mandates. And what are God's mandates to the angels according to this passage? To do His word and to do His pleasure. Let's take an in-depth look at each of these.

## Angels Hearken to God's Word

When the Bible says angels heed, or hearken, to the voice of God's Word, it doesn't mean they listen only when God speaks the Word; they also hearken when we speak it. Angels are listening to our words, waiting to take action when they hear us speak the Word of God. So the question is, what are we saying? Do the words that come from our mouths get the angels' attention, or do our words cause the angels simply to fold their wings and stand down?

God spoke through the prophet Isaiah, saying, *"So shall My word be that goes forth from My mouth; it shall not return to Me void, but it shall accomplish what I please, and it shall prosper in the thing for which I sent it"* (Isaiah 55:11). How does God's Word return to Him? When it comes from our mouths. I told the story in chapter 2 about my daughter Terri's fingertips being severed when she was a young child. When I took her to the restroom to wash her hand, I held her in one arm and opened the Bible with my free hand to Isaiah 55:11. I pointed to that verse and declared, "Lord, You said Your Word does not return to You void. I'm now returning Your Word to You." I then began quoting one scripture after another that promised healing and restoration for me and my seed.

It takes you and it takes me to return God's Word to Him. The angels are not responsible to return God's Word to Him; rather, they are to take heed to His Word—when we speak it. Notice the Bible quotation above says God's Word will not return void. This word *void* has three meanings: (1) without having any effect; (2) to be declared invalid; and (3) to take away its force or power. God intends that we understand the angels go into action when they hear us speak the Word of God; they excel in strength as they bring the Word to pass in our lives, never allowing its force to be removed so that it returns invalid and without having any effect.

I particularly like the way The Message renders Isaiah 55:11: *So will the words that come out of my mouth not come back empty-handed. They'll do the work I sent them to do, they'll complete the assignment I gave them.* God's Word has an assignment; every promise He makes has an assignment. The way we appropriate His promises in our lives is by speaking them. According to the book of Genesis, God made us in His image. Some older translations of Scripture refer to mankind as "speaking spirits." Unlike other forms of created life, human beings have the ability to speak—and God has instructed us what to speak. We are to speak the Word of God and expect the assignment on those words to be fulfilled.

The Bible says, *For the word of God is living and powerful, and sharper than any two-edged sword* (Hebrews 4:12). The Amplified Bible says, *For the Word that God speaks is alive and full of power [making it active, operative, energizing, and effective].* We are to be speaking God's powerful, active, and energizing Word, not just when we are in church, but all the time. Sadly, this is where some believers miss it when it comes to appropriating God's promises in their lives.

I remember the time Carolyn asked me to stop at the grocery store on the way home from the office to pick up a few items she needed to prepare dinner. I don't really like to go grocery shopping, because stores don't always keep items in the same location and it takes me extra time to find them. I was walking up and down the aisles that evening when I noticed two women who attended our church, just ahead of me. They hadn't yet noticed me, but I was close enough to hear the lady pushing the cart say to her friend as she picked up an item, "Have you seen the price of this? My goodness, I don't know what we're going to do; we can't afford this anymore."

The other lady said, "Oh, you haven't been to the meat section yet; the prices have really gone up. I told my husband we can no longer afford some of the cuts of meats he enjoys."

That's when they turned and saw me. "Oh, Brother Jerry, isn't

God good?" they said.

Yes, God is good; however, He is also true to His Word, which does not return to Him void. Instead of those ladies declaring, "My God will supply all my need according to His riches in glory by Christ Jesus," words the angels would have hearkened to and performed, they actually prevented the angels from fulfilling their assignment by saying, "We can't afford this." It is this kind of talk the apostle Paul refers to when he says, Let no corrupt communication proceed out of your mouth (Ephesians 4:29). The Amplified Bible calls this kind of communication "worthless talk."

Sadly, many Christians spend most of their time speaking worthless words that angels are not assigned to assist them with. Jesus used another term for these worthless words; He referred to them as "idle words" (see Matthew 12:36). The Message translation says "careless words," and the Amplified Bible further defines them as "inoperative, non-working words." So any words we speak outside the Word of God, particularly those that are in line with the way the world speaks, are considered inoperative, non-working, careless words that restrict angels from fulfilling their assignments.

Angels hearken to the Word of God to bring it to pass in our lives. That's why the psalmist said, *Let the words of my mouth and the meditation of my heart be acceptable in Your sight, O Lord, my strength and my Redeemer* (Psalms 19:14).

## Angels Do God's Pleasure

According to Psalms 103, not only do angels hearken to God's Word, they also do His pleasure. When the Bible speaks in this instance of God's pleasure, it means His will, His desire, and His plans for our lives.

The Bible sums up God's will for our lives in this one sentence: *If they obey and serve Him, they shall spend their days in prosperity, and their years in pleasure* (Job 36:11). Some folks get upset when they see God's people doing just that: spending our days in prosperity and our years in pleasure. As far as I'm concerned, their opinion doesn't matter; I'm not out to please man—I'm out to please God!

Notice the condition we must meet before we can experience God's promised prosperity and pleasure: we must obey and serve Him. If my prospering brings God pleasure, then I'm going to bring Him pleasure. I'm going to obey and serve Him.

The Word of God says, *Let them shout for joy and be glad, who favor my righteous cause; and let them say continually, "Let the Lord be magnified, who has pleasure in the prosperity of His servant"* (Psalms 35:27). The Bible again confirms that God receives pleasure when we prosper; such pleasure is true of any good father. After all, what kind of father gets upset when his children prosper?

My youngest daughter's ministry is just exploding all around the world, and I praise God for it. Terri's ministry moved into some beautiful offices in Rockwall, Texas, right on the lake, and within a year God had blessed the ministry so much that they had to hire more people and secure more space. I'll never say, "Terri, I'm so disappointed in you." No! She hears from me—via email, text, and telephone—telling her how much pleasure it gives me to see her prosper. I constantly rejoice with her.

My eldest daughter, Jerriann, has her own ministry that is also doing very well. She still has three children at home, so she doesn't travel as much as Terri does, but the Lord has nonetheless blessed her. Jerriann and Kellie Copeland grew up together and are like sisters. They now have their own television program, *The Kellie and Jerri Show*, on BVOVN, and it's doing extremely well. I'm not upset about their ministry's success; I tell them all the time how proud I am of them.

If either of my daughters' ministries grew to the point that it surpassed mine, it wouldn't bother me in the least. I would rejoice in all of the extraordinary manifestations of God's greatness in their lives.

Just as the prosperity of my daughters gives me pleasure, so the prosperity of God's servants gives Him pleasure. He has given the angels the assignment of bringing His Word concerning prosperity to pass; however, they are bound and restricted from doing so if we do not give voice to His Word. That's why Psalms 35:27 says, "Let them say *continually*." It's not enough to declare the Word once and expect the angels to bring it to pass. People who are always ill didn't talk about sickness and disease only one time; these people talked about their ill health continually. Likewise, people who end up in want and lack didn't talk about lack and want only one time; these people talked about it continually.

You may wonder, *How in the world can I possibly speak the Word of God continually?* The Bible says, *For out of the abundance of the heart [the] mouth speaks* (Matthew 12:34; Luke 6:45). Once you get the Word of God into your heart in abundance, you won't have any problem in speaking it continually. The Bible says, "Let them say continually," so let's speak the Word of God continually and let the angels do their job.

Third John 2 also affirms God's desire that we prosper: *Beloved, I pray that you may prosper in all things and be in health, just as your soul prospers.* From Genesis through Revelation, the Bible presents God's will for our prosperity. When people say prosperity isn't God's will, they don't understand the covenant God made with Abraham, who was very rich in livestock, silver, and gold (see Genesis 13:2). His prosperity lasted throughout his entire life, for the Bible says, *Now Abraham was old, well advanced in age; and the Lord had blessed Abraham in all things* (Genesis 25:8).

Prosperity was part of the old covenant, and it is part of the new covenant, which is a better covenant based on better promises (see Hebrews 8:6). If angels are to be involved in the prosperity God wants us to enjoy, then we have to be deliberate about what comes out of our mouths, because our angels are listening.

Jesus said, *"For by your words you will be justified, and by your words you will be condemned"* (Matthew 12:37). The Message translation says, *"Words are powerful; take them seriously."* Job received this revelation and said to God, *"Teach me, and I will hold my tongue; cause me to understand wherein I have erred. How forceful are right words!* (Job 6:24–25). After Job went through his tragedy, it dawned on him his words had something to do with it. We know this because he said, *"For the thing I greatly feared has come upon me"* (Job 3:25).

Fear is a spiritual force in the same way faith is a spiritual force. Just as we release faith by our words, so we release fear by our words. Evidently Job was talking all the time about what he feared, until he realized his words had everything to do with his circumstances. That's when he said he would hold his tongue and he asked the Lord to teach him and make him understand where he had erred.

It is God's intent that we spend our days in prosperity and our years in pleasure. The angels are already mandated to do God's pleasure, but it is up to us to activate them with our words.

### Seedtime and Harvest

God's number one way of bringing prosperity into our lives is through our appropriating the law of seedtime and harvest. God established this law in the book of Genesis when He said, *"While the earth remains, seedtime and harvest … shall not cease"* (Genesis 8:22). This law is still operative and it is still in force today.

Paul picks up on this fact in the New Testament when he says, *Do not be deceived, God is not mocked; for whatever a man sows, that he will also reap* (Galatians 6:7). The Phillips translation says, A man's harvest in life will depend entirely on what he sows. I've

## Angels in Our Financial Harvest

proven this truth in my own life and ministry, and I've seen it in the lives of my partners.

I remember a lady who came up to me one day in Meridian, Mississippi, during the early days of my ministry. She told me that her husband had passed away and she was living on a pension, a little bit of money that came to her from the job he'd had. When I finished the meeting that week, she stopped me on my way out and said, "Brother Jerry, I want to be your partner. I'm going to send you one dollar every month for the rest of my life."

I felt bad about taking that dollar from this lady, so I said, "Ma'am, this is so kind of you, and I appreciate it, but I'd feel badly if I took your dollar. You need it."

She was about seventy-five years old and probably wasn't five feet tall. But she put her hands on her hips and said, "Don't you practice what you preach, boy?"

"Yes, ma'am, I do," I said.

"No you don't! I'm on a fixed income; I'm trying to get off of it, and you're blocking my harvest."

I said, "Give me that dollar, lady!" And then she sent me one dollar each and every month for the rest of her life, which turned out to be years.

About twenty years later I was in Mississippi, at a meeting when a woman who was in her late forties or early fifties came up to me and said, "You don't know me, but I know you because you knew my mother."

"Who was your mother?" I asked. When she told me her mother's name, I recognized her as the little lady who'd sent me the dollar each month for years. "Oh yeah," I said. "Your mother was a sweetheart. She started partnering with me the first time I went to Meridian, and she partnered with me for a dollar each month until she went home to be with the Lord."

The lady smiled and said, "I know that. I wanted you to know my mother's partnership with you for that dollar each month made me a wealthy woman."

"How's that?" I asked.

"Well, Dad died, and the property the family owned went to my mother. I'm an only child, so when my mother died, the property went to me. We used the acreage for farming—until the city where we live decided it needed our property. They wanted to do some expansion, and and wanted to buy it from me and now I'm a wealthy woman because of that dollar my mother sent you every month!"

The Bible says, *And let us not be weary in well doing: for in due season we shall reap, if we faint not* (Galatians 6:9). God honored that woman's sowing, which determined her daughter's future. Through the law of seedtime and harvest, that daughter became a wealthy woman when she reaped a financial harvest off of the seed her mother had sown. I like the way the Amplified Bible translates God's Word about sowing and reaping:

> [Remember] this: he who sows sparingly and grudgingly will also reap sparingly and grudgingly, and he who sows generously [that blessings may come to someone] will also reap generously and with blessings.
>
> Let each one [give] as he had made up his own mind and purposed in his heart, not reluctantly or sorrowfully or under compulsion, for God loves (He takes pleasure in, prizes above other things, and is unwilling to abandon or to do without) a cheerful (joyous, "prompt to do it") giver [whose heart is in his giving].
>
> And God is able to make all grace (every favor and earthly blessing) come to you in abundance, so that you may always and under all circumstances and whatever the need be self-sufficient [possessing enough to require no aid or support and furnished in abundance for every good work and charitable donation] (2 Corinthians 9:6–8).

Although that little woman in Mississippi had only one dollar to sow each month, she sowed generously, without sorrow or feeling pressured to do so. As a result, not only did God supply the woman's needs for the rest of her life, but her daughter also reaped a bountiful harvest from the seed her mother had sown.

It's obvious God intends for us to have a harvest from every seed we sow. Harvesting is His will, His plan, and it brings Him pleasure when we prosper. The angels have a mandate to hearken to God's Word and do His pleasure; however, we have an enemy who is consumed with keeping us from experiencing God's best. He wants to block our harvest. Jesus identified Satan as a thief, saying, *The thief does not come except to steal, and to kill, and to destroy. I have come that they may have life, and that they may have it more abundantly* (John 10:10).

Satan wants to hold back our financial harvest in the same way he attempted to hold back the harvest of Daniel's prayers. After three weeks of prayer and fasting, Daniel had a vision of a man clothed in linen, whose waist was girded with gold, who said, *"Do not fear, Daniel, for from the first day ... your words were heard; and I have come because of your words. But the prince of the kingdom of Persia withstood me twenty-one days; and behold, Michael, one of the chief princes, came to help me* (Daniel 10:12–13). Notice it was an angel who hearkened to Daniel's words and came in answer to his prayers.

When it comes to harvesting our seed, we don't have to sit back and allow the enemy to steal or withhold the prosperity God has planned for us. It is this prosperity that will fund His gospel being preached to all the world. In the book of James we see an analogy of how Satan attempts to hold back our harvest.

> Come now, you rich, weep and howl for your miseries that are coming upon you! Your riches are corrupted, and your garments will be moth-eaten. Your gold and silver are

corroded, and their corrosion will be a witness against you and eat your flesh like fire. You have heaped treasure in the last days. Indeed the wages of the laborers who mowed your fields, which you kept back by fraud, cry out; and the cries of the reapers have reached the ears of the Lord of Sabaoth (James 5:1–4).

Notice the setting is "the last days" and this wealthy, yet corrupt man is holding back the wages due those who earned them. It's interesting the Bible uses the word *fraud*, which means "deception" and "trickery." Aren't those the exact same tactics the enemy uses to hold back our financial harvest? But let's take a look at the words that reached the Lord of Sabaoth—the Lord of hosts!

**Cries for the Harvest**

The words that reached the ears of the Lord of hosts (the Lord of angels) came from two sources. One source was the reapers; the other, the wages themselves. Consequently, if wages (finances) are a part of our harvest, then both our cries and the cries of those wages have reached God's ears.

Anytime we sow seed according to the authority of God's Word, we are entitled to the harvest the seed produces. If that harvest isn't coming in, then it is crying out, saying that we are its rightful owners.

Sometimes I get up in the morning, cup my hand around my ear, and say, "Carolyn, do you hear that?" She always smiles because she knows what I will say next: "That's the sound of our harvest crying out to us. It's saying, 'I belong to you; you're my rightful owner.'"

Again, in our scriptural analogy we see two cries going forth: one from the harvest, the other from the rightful owners. Let's look again at who hears these cries: the Lord of Sabaoth, or "the Lord of hosts." Remember, the words *hosts* and *angels* are interchangeable; therefore, the cries enter the ears of the Lord of the angels! This means we have harvesting angels working in our behalf; as we speak the Word of God over our harvest, they hearken to that Word and bring in the harvest the enemy is holding back. Remember, God heard Daniel's cries the first day he prayed, but the enemy withstood Daniel until the angel Michael came to help Daniel out.

The angels, who are ministering spirits sent to assist us, are waiting for our cry. The word *cry* as it is used in James 5 has nothing to do with tears: it actually means "a loud utterance in protest and opposition." To cry also implies a demand for immediate action.

If you've been standing in faith for your harvest but it is being withheld, then you may not be doing enough. When you send forth a biblical cry protesting and opposing the enemy who is withholding your harvest—a loud cry demanding immediate action—your words enter the ears of the Lord of Sabaoth. If necessary, He will release a legion of angels to get that harvest into your hands.

The Bible says, *The Lord of hosts is with us* (Psalm 46:11), and *Praise Him, all His angels; praise Him, all His hosts!* (Psalm 148:11). The angels, the hosts of the Lord, are assigned to work in our behalf, but it is up to us to appropriate them. Some angels have specific assignments. Harvesting angels assist in the harvest of both souls and the financial seed we sow. When we cry out for the harvest, knowing our financial harvest is also crying out for us, we can be assured we're not alone. The angels hear the Word coming from our mouths, and they hearken to it—they go into action. Even if it takes some time, we must never give up, because in due season we will reap our harvest.

I want to point out again that although God's Word promises if we obey Him, we will spend our days in prosperity and our years in pleasure, the primary purpose of our harvest is so that the gospel can be preached in all the world. Not only will people be drawn to God when they hear the gospel, but when they see us prospering in the midst of a bad economy or a world in turmoil, they will want to know the God we serve.

Do not give up on speaking God's Word continually, for in so doing, you are giving strength to the angels God sends to win the battle over your harvest. The Bible says, *You will also declare a thing, and it will be established for you; so light will shine on your ways* (Job 22:28). Therefore, I invite you to join me in this declaration as we demand immediate action for our financial harvest:

> Satan, in the name of Jesus, I command you to release my financial harvest, which is rightfully mine according to the authority of God's Word. I refuse to allow you to hold back my harvest; I refuse to allow you to keep it from me; I refuse to allow you to steal it from me. The Lord of hosts is backing me right now. His angels are instructed to assist me in laying hold of what rightfully belongs to me.
>
> Angels, I release you to go and war over my financial harvest. I'm crying out, and I'll not be satisfied until my harvest is in my hands. Angels, gather it up and see to it that it comes. I'm believing in "suddenlies" in Jesus's name, and I will not quit. I will not give up, and I will not grow weary.
>
> Thank You, Lord, for watching over Your Word to perform it in my behalf. I receive it and consider it done in Jesus' name.
>
> Amen.

# PART 3
## Engaging with the Prophetic Word

*"Believe in the Lord your God, and you shall be established; believe His prophets, and you shall prosper"*
*— 2 Chronicles 20:20*

# CHAPTER 7
## Wage the Good Warfare

Many years ago I dreamed of a time when I would to go churches to preach and, because of God's favor and blessing on my life, I'd have the ability to pay off their mortgages before I left town. I have actually paid off such mortgages on multiple occasions, and I expect to do so again and again. Please understand that I only do this when and where the Holy Spirit leads me to do so.

The more harvest that comes into my hands, the more I'm able to do for the body of Christ and the kingdom of God. I know many believers who would say the same thing; however, Satan is not going to roll over and play dead, and allow us to have an abundant harvest, without putting up a fight. The enemy is consistent in his assignment to steal, kill, and destroy, but are we equally consistent in the part we play in bringing in our financial harvest? Do we have a determined and aggressive attitude when it comes to our harvest?

In the early days of my ministry before I had my first airplane, I drove to the cities where I'd been invited to preach. I was on my way through Oklahoma to Kansas one day in May during the season of the wheat harvest. Fields that ran as far as I could see on both sides of the highway promised a great harvest. The wheat stalks waving in the gentle wind looked like waves on an ocean. It was a beautiful sight.

I'd decided I would leave immediately after the evening service, make the three-hour drive to Oklahoma City to spend the night, and then return to Fort Worth the following morning. Driving south on Interstate 35 under the dark late-spring sky, I saw two distant headlights in the wheat field to my right. A lone combine was harvesting wheat. As I watched the headlights and pondered the driver who had chosen to work through the night to reap his harvest, the Lord said, "That's an aggressive harvester. If you'll take the same position with the seeds you've sown, you'll see a greater harvest than you've ever seen before."

Until that time I'd always been an aggressive sower, but I'd never thought about being an aggressive harvester. I knew the things God had called me to do required that I have an airplane and that I was not to have any debt on it. I knew I was to help churches pay off their mortgages and to preach the gospel in all the world. Doing all this, and more, would require a greater level of harvest than I'd yet experienced in my life. It would also require a greater level of faith than I'd walked in previously.

In the apostle Paul's first letter to Timothy, whom he considered a son in the faith, he wrote these words to his young protégé: *This charge I commit to you, son Timothy, according to the prophecies previously made concerning you, that by them you may wage the good warfare* (1 Timothy 1:18). The Passion translation says, *With this encouragement use your prophecies as weapons as you wage spiritual warfare by faith and with a clean conscience.* In other words, we take our faith to another level when we use the prophecies concerning us as weapons of warfare!

You may say, "Wait a minute, Brother Jerry, what if I haven't had any prophecies spoken over me where my harvest is concerned?" In Bible days prophetic words typically came from God through the word of a prophet; however, not all prophetic words come directly through the mouth of a modern-day prophet. Bible prophecies, many of which apply to us today, were initially spoken through the mouths of prophets. These prophecies now come to us through the written Word of God.

Jesus was recognized as a prophet throughout His earthly ministry. Although He addressed His words to those who were with Him, He was also speaking prophetically of what He saw in the Spirit when He said, *"The harvest truly is great, but the laborers are few: therefore pray the Lord of the harvest to send out laborers into His harvest!"* (Luke 10:2). Notice Jesus used the word great when He described the harvest. In the original language this word also means "abundant." The prophetic word Jesus spoke is relevant for us today; we can use it to wage good warfare in behalf of the abundant harvest that belongs to us.

In the twenty-eighth chapter of Deuteronomy, we find a list of blessings that belong to God's people. However, these blessings come with a condition: *And all these blessings shall come upon you and overtake you because you obey the voice of the Lord* (Deuteronomy 28:2). Our obedience is the key to blessings overtaking us. One of the Hebrew meanings of the word overtake is "surprise." We learned in chapter 2 that God is famous for His surprises, and I've found this to be true in my life—especially where being aggressive about reaping an abundant harvest is concerned.

For instance, I've been a classic car enthusiast all of my life. It wasn't an acquired taste for me; I was born with it. When I owned Jerry's Paint and Body Shop, one of the things I did was restore classic automobiles. I loved the challenge of bringing those old relics back to life; nonetheless, after I closed down the business and went into ministry, I was totally submitted to what God wanted me to do. Working on cars was no longer my desire.

But many years later the Lord said, "Son, I want you to use your passion for classic cars and motorcycles as a tool for evangelism." I understood what He meant because I could relate to those who were in the business. I knew that, for many of the guys in the classic car, hot rod, and racecar businesses, their cars were their gods.

I now have a wonderful collection of classic cars, which I take to car shows so that God can use me to minister to people. When people come around my cars and want to talk to me, they don't know I'm a preacher. However, I've prayed for people with cancer while at a car show, and they were healed.

I remember walking into my shop one day years ago and looking at my collection of four classic cars and two classic motorcycles. I said, "Lord, I just want You to know that none of this means anything to me other than the fact that You've blessed me with it. But I want to show You that You're still number one in my life. I'm going to sow these cars and motorcycles, and I'd like You to tell me where to sow them." Then I sowed them as He instructed.

I reaped an abundant harvest on those vehicles I'd sown as seeds. After some time had passed, Carolyn said to me one day as she was looking at my greatly-expanded collection, "Jerry, don't you ever sow all of your cars and motorcycles again."

"Why not?" I asked.

"Anytime you sow cars or motorcycles, they come back to you in fleets. Now you have so many that you'll have to build a bigger garage to hold them."

I've always enjoyed classic cars and motorcycles, but today I use them as a tool for evangelism. And I'm continually harvesting from the seed I sow.

I remember one day in particular when Carolyn and I took Richard and Lindsay Roberts to lunch. Carolyn was driving, and I was in the back seat with Richard when I got a text. It said, "Brother Jerry, I'm one of your partners. I've heard you talk about the '65 GTO you owned before going into the ministry and how much you enjoyed that car before having to sell it so Carolyn would have money while you were in military training. I have a rare model restored '65 GTO, and I want to bless you with it. Are you interested?"

In my spirit I heard the Lord say *surprise!*

That car is now part of my collection. It's so immaculate that I could eat off the engine. Every time I walk by it, I hear God say *surprise!* He's the God of marvels, the God of wonders. Do you suppose the wonder of my receiving that car had anything to do with my sowing?

I remember another time God performed a similar wonder in my life. On my flight to the one of Brother Copeland's Believers' Conventions, I read a magazine article about two men who were in World War II together. While they were in the military, they rode Harleys together and became close friends. After the war they continued to ride Harleys, and eventually they each opened Harley-Davidson dealerships in the cities where they lived.

One day they got together, and one of them said, "I wonder what happened to those fifty Harleys that were sent to Russia in crates during the war and put in a warehouse." After doing some research, the men discovered those motorcycles were still in their unopened crates in a warehouse in Russia. So they made arrangements to buy them all and have them shipped to the US. However, somehow the people learned about the motorcycles and confiscated all but three of them, which the men eventually received. They each took one motorcycle and gave the third Harley to a friend.

As I read the article I thought, *Wouldn't it be awesome to have a Harley that had actually been in World War II?*

I preached at the convention Thursday night as I usually do and then went back to the hotel. The next morning a staff member came to me and said, "We got an envelope in the offering last night that has your name on it," and he handed it to me. I opened it and pulled out a note that said, "I know you like classic motorcycles and you like Harley Davidsons. I have one and it's a military Harley, but I turned it into a civilian bike. It's torn apart, but everything is painted, and it's ready to be reassembled. If you would like to have it, I would like to sow it into your ministry." He then signed his name and listed his phone number. I called him, and thanked him and arranged to pick it up and bring it back to Fort Worth.

Long story short, I had the pieces brought to Texas in boxes, which I delivered to a friend of mine in Austin who restores all of my classic Harleys. He did the research and discovered it was one of the bikes that came from Russia and it's now sitting in my shop with all of its military markings perfectly restored. Every time I walk by, I marvel as I hear God say *surprise!*

Now what are the odds of my reading that magazine article and then the following week my being blessed with one of those motorcycles? When someone says, "Things like that don't just happen, Brother Jerry," I say, "They do to me!"

I am convinced my abundant harvesting is a direct result of my sowing. I wouldn't have these testimonies of the extraordinary manifestations of God's greatness if I weren't an abundant sower and an aggressive harvester.

And while God has promised that if we obey Him, we will spend our days in prosperity and our years in pleasure, the purpose of our harvest is always to bring glory to Him.

### We Determine Our Harvest

An abundant harvest doesn't just happen. If I wasn't a sower, then God would have to violate His own Word to give me an abundant harvest. He is the one who established the principle of sowing and reaping when He said, *"While the earth remains, seedtime and harvest, cold and heat, winter and summer, and day and night shall not cease"* (Genesis 8:22). Planet Earth is still here; therefore, the law of seedtime and harvest is still in effect.

The Word of God says, *Do not be deceived, God is not mocked: for whatever a man sows, that he will also reap* (Galatians 6:7). This verse teaches us that we each determine our own harvest through the seed we sow. I can't determine your harvest, and you can't determine mine.

When the Bible says God is not *mocked*, it means He is will not be "ridiculed" or "treated with contempt." The word *contempt* means "showing no respect for." In other words, when someone says, "I don't believe my sowing or my words have anything to do with the outcome," that person's words demonstrate contempt because they show no respect for God and His Word. Talking this way will not produce an abundant harvest. The Phillips translation of Galatians 6:7 says, *A man's harvest in life will depend entirely on what he sows.*

Jerry Savelle Ministries International is governed by a board of directors, and most of those directors have served in our ministry for nearly forty years. We hold our annual board meeting in January of each year to go over our financial statements and discuss the vision and plans the Lord has given me for the upcoming year. The last thing the board does before dismissing is to hold a compensation committee meeting to determine Carolyn's and my salary for the upcoming year.

Carolyn and I are not part of this meeting. We don't tell board members what to do, and we don't leave any hints about this aspect of the ministry. The board approaches the matter from a legal basis according to IRS standards; our attorney investigates other corporations that bring in the same amount of money to see what their top-echelon management team is paid. Once the board members have made their determination, they call us into the room and let us know what our salary will be.

When they tell us what our compensation will be for the upcoming year, I tell them, "Gentlemen, Carolyn and I appreciate your generosity and your love for us over the years. But I want you to know that even though this is my salary, that I'm paid out of Jerry Savelle Ministries International, it will not be my total income. My income will far exceed this amount, because I don't live on a salary. I live on my giving, and I live on my sowing."

What am I doing when I say this? I am taking the prophetic

Word of God that says *"All these blessings will come upon you and overtake you"* (Deuteronomy 28:2), and waging good warfare with it, as Paul instructed Timothy to do. Though my board can set my salary, those directors never determine my annual income. Every year the amount of income I report to the IRS is far more than my salary. I'm in charge of my own financial destiny, and you are in charge of yours.

### Overcoming Financial Famine

The Bible says, *But this I say: He who sows sparingly will also reap sparingly, and he who sows bountifully will also reap bountifully* (2 Corinthians 9:6). Paul wrote these words under the inspiration of the Holy Ghost, but it was God who established this principle. To sow sparingly is to sow modestly, seldom, or infrequently. According to God's laws, if we sow bountifully, then we will reap a bountiful harvest.

When people say, "Times are hard, Brother Jerry. How can I be sure that if I sow, I'll get a harvest?" I always think of the biblical account of Isaac. He lived in a day when famine was so severe in the land that he considered going to Egypt. But the Lord told him to stay where he was and He would bless him. The Bible says, *Then Isaac sowed in that land, and reaped in the same year a hundredfold; and the Lord blessed him. The man began to prosper, and continued prospering until he became very prosperous* (Genesis 26:12-13). It looks to me as though the result of Isaac's obedience was that he spent his days in prosperity—and everyone else in the land saw the blessing of God upon his life.

I was with Brother Copeland in 1981 at the Charlotte, North Carolina, Believers' Convention when I had a supernatural visitation from the Lord. It was the first time I'd experienced such a visitation.

We'd been there several days and had attended all of the services.

I'd just finished preaching an afternoon session, and Carolyn and I had returned to our hotel room to rest. She said, "Are you going to take a nap before we go back to listen to Brother Copeland preach tonight?" I told her I was just going to sit in the living room of our suite and relax, so she went into the bedroom to take a nap.

I'd just sat down on the sofa, placed my feet on the coffee table, and leaned back when suddenly the Lord appeared. The shekinah glory filled the room to the point that I couldn't see the furniture.

At this particular time in 1981, a financial crisis that affected almost the entire world was also impacting the body of Christ. The economy was bad, the oil industry looked as if it would collapse, rumors of bank insolvency were rampant, and money was scarce. However, these facts didn't seem to bother the Lord. When His presence filled the room, He said, "I'm going to reveal to you the keys to overcoming financial famine." As soon as He began to speak, I reached over and picked up my legal pad and pen from the coffee table. I don't know how long He spoke, but I wrote everything He said to me.

When Carolyn woke from her nap and came into the living room, she immediately sensed the glory and said, "What's going on in here?"

"I just had a visitation from the Lord," I told her.

She sat down, and we basked together in the glory of the Lord for some time. When she asked if I would tell Brother Copeland what had just happened I said, "No, he will pick up on it in the Spirit."

Carolyn and I arrived at the service that evening and took our seats on the front row along with Charles and Peggy Caps and Norvel Hayes; Gloria Copeland was seated next to me. Usually when Brother Copeland steps up to the pulpit to preach, he says, "Let's open our Bibles tonight to ..." and then he tells us where to turn. That night all he said was, "Let's open our Bibles." He paused, then looked at me and said, "Jerry, God visited you today and He wants you to take this service. Come up here." So I preached the message God had given me that afternoon on how to overcome the financial famine. The title was "Sowing in Famine."

During His visitation that afternoon, one of the things the Lord had said to me was, "I want you to write a check for an amount totaling $1,000 from each outreach of your ministry as well as another $1,000 from your personal account, and I want you to sow these checks into Brother Copeland's ministry tonight." We had ten major departments in the ministry, so the funds from the ministry equaled $10,000. With the addition of another $1,000 of our personal money, the checks I wrote totaled $11,000.

At the conclusion of my message, I told the people what the Lord had instructed me to do in preparation to sow during famine. I sowed that check to Brother Copeland's ministry, and I challenged the people to pray and then do likewise. As a result of our obedience to the Lord's instructions, we had a miracle-breakthrough offering that night. It could only be described as a marvel, a wonder, and an extraordinary manifestation of God's greatness.

The following month I was with Kenneth Hagin in one of his meetings. He was on the platform preaching, but then he stopped in the middle of his sermon and said, "Brother Jerry, stand up. God just told me to do something I've never done before. I'm going to sow the largest seed I've ever sown: I'm giving you my airplane." Part of the seed I'd sown the previous week had come from my aviation department; at the time, I was believing for my next airplane. It turned out that the value of Brother Hagin's airplane was more than one hundred times the value of what I'd sown.

At the next night's session of the same meeting, a couple came to Carolyn and me following the service, handed us an envelope, and said, "The Lord told us to sow $100,000 into your television ministry, so we're giving you this check that He said to bring with us." In two consecutive evenings two of our ministry departments reaped a hundred-fold return on the seed we had sown, just as Isaac had done when he had obeyed God and sown in famine. By December of 1981 we had received a hundred-fold return on every seed we had sown from the ten departments in our ministry and from our personal seed as well.

Something else significant happened prior to the end of 1981. Brother Copeland and Gloria were going to be in Philadelphia for one of their three-day meetings, and because Carolyn and I didn't have anything scheduled on those dates, we decided to attend. When I called Brother Copeland and told him Carolyn and I would be there to sit in the services and enjoy the Word, he said, "Jerry, there's no need for both of us to fly our airplanes; you and Carolyn can come with us." So we flew with them to Philadelphia.

I was looking forward to hearing Brother Copeland preach, but Friday morning he called me and said, "I want you to do the service this morning." I preached the message, "Sowing in Famine," and when I finished, I turned to walk off the platform. That's when Brother Copeland said, "Wait a minute, Jerry. The Word of the Lord has come to me," and he began to prophesy over me. It was a lengthy prophecy; some of the things he said by the Holy Ghost were so phenomenal that I couldn't wrap my mind around them. But my spirit took them in.

When Brother Copeland finished prophesying over me, I said, "I receive it by faith"—and then I went straight to his sound technician and said, "Please get me a copy of that prophecy as quickly as you can." When I got back to my office, I had the prophetic word transcribed. My art department then created a nice poster that I had framed and hung on the wall in my office.

One part of that prophecy said, "And God is going to turn over to you some exceedingly valuable property." The Bible says, *You shall also decide and decree a thing, and it will be established for you; and the light [of God's favor] will shine upon your ways* (Job 22:28). Every time I walked into my office, I'd lay my hands on that framed poster and declare, "I decree it, and I receive it!" What was I doing? I was taking the prophetic word that was spoken over me, and I was waging a good warfare with it.

Right across the road from our headquarters in Crowley, Texas, were over one hundred acres of undeveloped property. The Lord said to me, "I will arrange for you to have as much of that land as you want for the price you want to pay—if you'll just be patient." My answer was, "Consider me patient now."

A short time later somebody bought that land, and an article in the Fort Worth Star Telegram described the plans for what would be built there. After I finished reading the article, I held up the newspaper and said, "Lord, did you read the paper this morning? Somebody bought my property."

"Whose report will you believe?" He asked. "Throw that paper in the trash where it belongs. I told you to be patient."

I understood the word *patient* means to be "consistent; never changing regardless of the circumstances." So I remained patient.

It turned out that company went bankrupt and another company bought the property. The second company also went bankrupt, and a third company bought the property. They too went bankrupt. One day we got a call from the government agency that had repossessed the property from the third owner. The man said, "You seem to be the only organization building successfully in that part of Fort Worth without going bankrupt. We don't want this property on our books anymore, and we'd like to invite you to make an offer. Just so you'll know, there's a $1.2 million lean against it, so you'll need to come up with a lot more than that."

The Lord had told me I would pay whatever I wanted to pay, so I called my attorney and said, "Wayne, do you remember me telling you what the Lord told me about paying whatever I wanted to pay for that land across the street from our headquarters?" When he said yes I said, "I've prayed, and what I want to pay for it is $200,000 cash. I want the lien removed, and I want clear title—with the mineral rights."

When Wayne called the agency in Washington, D.C., his opening remarks were, "Do you believe in miracles?"

"No," they said, "We work for the government. We don't see miracles."

"Well, I believe in miracles, and my client believes in miracles. Here's the offer: He'll give you $200,000 cash. He wants the lien removed, and he wants a clear title. He also wants the mineral rights."

Total silence.

"Are you still there?" Wayne asked.

"Yes, but that offer is so ridiculous, I'm not even going to report it," the man replied.

Wayne said, "Your superiors told you to call Mr. Savelle, and I've just given you his offer. I'll expect to hear from you by the end of the day." Then he hung up.

When the man called Wayne back later that same day, his opening statement was, "We now believe in miracles." We paid $200,000 cash. We got the lien removed. We got a clear title, and we also got the mineral rights.

The problem was, nothing about that undeveloped property looked like the exceedingly valuable property that was prophesied in 1981. We purchased it with future growth in mind; however, the God of marvels, wonders, and extraordinary manifestations of His greatness had taken over. It wasn't long before gas wells were discovered on the property.

The $200,000 I paid for that piece of property quickly produced $3 million in royalties. To get the gas from the property to the plant, the oil-and-gas company had to install pipelines on the property, for which the company paid us $450,000. When gas was discovered on the surrounding residential properties, they asked if they could use our property for a drilling-pad site, for which the company offered me a royalty from the other property owners' royalties. My first royalty check was for $350,000.

Just recently, I sold a fraction of my property for $1.5 million. One of the major developers in south Fort Worth came to me and said, "I'm a developer, and I tried to buy this piece of property for the longest time but couldn't. You're a preacher, and you got it. I want to know how you did it."

"It's the favor of God," I said.

"No, really. Who do you know?"

When I said God, he didn't want to accept my answer and left. But it wasn't long before he returned. This time he said, "I'd like to know your God."

When the world sees us living our days in prosperity and experiencing a lifetime of pleasure, they will want to know our God. We are the ones who determine the size of the harvest we receive according to the seed we sow. And when we wage a good warfare according to both the spoken and written prophecies that are ours to lay hold of, we can be assured that the harvest will be abundant.

# CHAPTER 8
## Prepared for the Harvest

Let's look again at the prophetic word Jesus spoke about the harvest: *"The harvest truly is great, but the laborers are few; therefore pray the Lord of the harvest to send out laborers into His harvest"* (Luke 10:2). We learned a great harvest is synonymous with an abundant harvest and that in the end times the angels will be involved with this harvest—both of souls and of the finances it takes to harvest these souls.

We also understand we have access to God's covenant of marvels, which He made with Moses, saying, *"Behold, I make a covenant. Before all your people I will do marvels such as have not been done in all the earth, nor in any nation; and all the people among whom you are shall see the work of the Lord. For it is an awesome thing that I will do with you"* (Exodus 34:10). God's purpose in performing marvels, wonders, and extraordinary manifestations of His greatness is not merely to bless us; ultimately, His purpose is to get the attention of a world that does not yet know Him.

Our God is a harvest-minded God; therefore, we are to be harvest-minded people. Becoming harvest-minded prepares us to receive the great harvest Jesus prophesied over two thousand years ago. When it comes to the harvest, where we sow our seed has everything to do with the outcome. I was still a child when I first learned this principle on the Mississippi farm where I was born.

My grandfather purchased the farm in 1927. The land was a self-sustaining environment that enabled my grandparents to make it through the Great Depression that began in 1929. My dad was raised on that farm, and a few years after I was born there, my parents moved us to Shreveport Louisiana. During my school years I often spent my summers at the farm, and I always loved going to the fields with my grandfather. At that time the farm was about seventy total acres, nearly half of which was planted with crops, the other half used for maintaining cattle and hogs.

I remember riding on the back of my grandfather's 1927 Massey Ferguson tractor as we headed to an area known as "the flat" to sow seed. Every year Grandpa would say, "Son, we're going to have a great crop this year."

I'd say, "Grandpa, you say that every year. How do you know we're going to have a great crop?"

"Son, this is good old Mississippi Delta soil. You can grow anything here."

Grandpa was right; it was good soil. In fact, agriculturalists tell us even now that the flooding of the Mississippi River over the years has brought nutrients and minerals from the north to the mouth of the Mississippi, making the soil there some of the richest and most fertile in the nation. Grandpa could have planted most anything in that soil and reaped an abundant harvest.

After I surrendered my life to the Lord and He began to teach me His Word, I envisioned my grandfather's farm when I read what Jesus had to say about the sower.

> "Listen! Behold, a sower went out to sow. And it happened, as he sowed, that some seed fell by the wayside; and the birds of the air came and devoured it. Some fell on stony ground, where it did not have much earth; and immediately it sprang up because it had no depth of earth. But when the sun was up it was scorched, and because it had no root it withered away. And some seed fell among the thorns; and the thorns grew up and choked it, and it yielded no crop.

But other seed fell on good ground and yielded a crop that sprang up, increased and produced: some thirtyfold, some sixty, and some a hundred" (Mark 4:3–8).

We understand Jesus used this parable to illustrate the Word of God as a seed sown into the heart of an individual. Jesus described each heart as one of four types of ground: by-the-wayside ground, stony ground, thorny ground, and good ground. Jesus then illustrated the direct relationship between the ground where a seed is sown and the size of the harvest. When it came to the harvest from good ground, He said, *"But these are the ones sown on good ground, those who hear the word, accept it, and bear fruit: some thirtyfold, some sixty, and some a hundred"* (verse 20).

Notice Jesus said seed sown on good ground has the ability to produce a hundredfold return. This huge return is the exact amount Isaac harvested when he sowed in obedience to God's instruction: *Then Isaac sowed in that land, and reaped in the same year a hundredfold* (Genesis 26:12).

When it comes to sowing our financial seed into good soil, the exact place we sow is of great importance. I remember the time Oral Roberts asked that I come to his office to spend the day with him. Our discussion that day was focused on the laws of sowing and reaping. Brother Roberts said, "Jerry, the Lord recently instructed me to redirect my seed."

I asked what he meant by that and he said, "I've been sowing into different ministries over the years, and some of them are no longer productive. Some have gotten into sin, some are not preaching the Word, and others are not living godly lives. Some are taking the money I send and doing things with it other than what they told me they would do. God is having me redirect my seed because He knows I must have a good harvest."

To keep the soil of my own ministry productive, I've endeavored to keep my life pure for the past fifty years. There's never been a scandal in either my personal life or my ministry. I've been faithful to God, my wife, my family, and my calling. I intend to keep the soil of my ministry as rich and fertile as the good-ole Mississippi-Delta soil I was raised on, because where we sow has everything to do with the kind of harvest we get.

Once a seed is sown, it has to germinate, or develop. The seed develops by putting forth shoots and sprouts. Jesus described the successful agricultural process from seedtime to harvest: *For the earth yields crops by itself: first the blade, then the head, after that the full grain in the head. But when the grain ripens, immediately he puts in the sickle, because the harvest has come"* (Mark 4:24). What would happen if that seed failed to germinate? There would be no harvest.

Agriculturalists often use the term *dormant*, a word some people may not be familiar with, although I learned it at an early age from my grandfather. Until a seed germinates, it is considered a "dormant seed." The seed will remain dormant until it is watered. While we cannot reap a harvest without first sowing a seed, and while where we sow a seed is critical to the kind of harvest we will reap, nothing is going to happen until we water our seed. Without water a seed will lie dormant in the ground. I think this is where many in the body of Christ miss it when it comes to operating successfully in the law of seedtime and harvest. It's where I once missed it.

I knew Jesus had prophesied a great harvest, and I knew that according to the Word of God it was possible to reap a hundredfold return on my seed. The Lord had spoken to me that night I saw the lone harvester in Kansas, saying, "If you'll take the same position with the seeds you've sown, you'll see a greater harvest." I was taking my prophecies and waging good warfare with them. I was also sowing generously and consistently into good ground. Even so, I wasn't reaping the kind of harvest I was believing for.

I'd done everything I knew to do, according to the Word of God, to prepare for the harvest; however, I wasn't watering my seed.

How are we to water our seed? Let's begin by looking to the book of Revelation as John describes Jesus: *His voice [was] as the sound of many waters* (Revelation 1:15). The Word that comes out of the mouth of Jesus is likened to water. Speaking of the relationship between Jesus and the body of Christ, the apostle Paul said, *Christ also loved the church and gave Himself for her, that He might sanctify and cleanse her with the washing of water by the word* (Ephesians 5:25–26). These passages are but two specific examples of the Word being likened unto water.

In addition, the Lord said through the prophet Isaiah, *"For as the rain comes down, and the snow from heaven, and do not return there, but water the earth, and make it bring forth and bud, that it may give seed to the sower and bread to the eater, so shall My word be that goes forth from My mouth; it shall not return to Me void, but it shall accomplish what I please and shall prosper in the thing for which I sent it"* (Isaiah 55:10–11). In other words, God Himself likens His Word unto water, which causes germination and growth.

Furthermore, Jesus said, *"He who believes in Me, as the Scripture has said, out of his heart will flow rivers of living water"* (John 7:38). He also said, *"For out of the abundance of the heart the mouth speaks"* (Matthew 12:34). This tells us that when we have God's Word in our hearts in abundance, it will flow like water out of our mouths. Jesus again affirmed this fact when He said, *"The words that I speak to you are spirit, and they are life"* (John 6:63). Finally, we find this truth in the book of Proverbs: *The words of a man's mouth are as deep waters, and the wellspring of wisdom as a flowing brook* (Proverbs 18:4).

Based on what the Scripture tells us, we water our seed by speaking the Word of God over it on a consistent basis.

Agriculturalists tell us that once a seed is sown it must be watered frequently; some say daily. But the problem with some in the body of Christ is that they are not consistent in watering their seed once it's sown. They may sow a financial seed in good ground and initially declare they will receive an abundant harvest, but after a few days they quit watering their seed with words of faith. "I sowed an abundant seed in good ground," they may say. That's good, but the question is, are they watering their seed?

It's been years since I was active in any kind of farming. These days, the most significant growth on our property takes place in Carolyn's flower garden. Yet if she's going to have an abundant harvest of the roses and agapanthus she enjoys so much, those plants have to be watered—not just once or every now and then, but frequently and consistently.

Don't allow the seed you sow to lie dormant, even in good ground; water it with the Word. And don't stop watering it once it comes up. Use your mouth to declare God's Word over your seed, and you will reap the abundant harvest you need so that you will not only be blessed but also be a blessing to others.

## The Purpose of the Blessing

I came to understand early in my walk with the Lord that I was to be a blessing to others. As the story goes, I asked the Lord, "What is Your definition of being a blessing as it pertains to me?" His answer had a profound impact on me. "I want you to be an instrument through which my divine favor flows toward another person, preventing misfortune and making their life better," He said. From then on, blessing others is what Carolyn and I have lived for. We want to bring them hope, to prevent misfortune, and to be an encouragement.

Carolyn and I both sow and harvest abundantly, yet we don't hoard up just for ourselves the blessing that comes from the harvest. I sometimes get letters from people who are angry about how blessed I am. Well, they'll just have to talk to God about that fact. I'm not going to say, "Lord, don't bless me anymore because some people don't like it." I'm going to continue sowing, harvesting, and being blessed because the more blessed I am, the greater instrument of blessing I can be to others.

When Carolyn and I first started walking in faith together, we didn't have the means to be a blessing. We had to believe God for the clothes on our backs, the food on our table, and gasoline for our vehicle—which we then had to believe would run once it had gas. Those who criticize us now weren't there to see us in the early days. There weren't there when we moved to Fort Worth and I walked the streets looking for Coke bottles to sell so that we would have money to buy food for our babies. Carolyn and I had made the commitment to trust God and live by faith; when we did as God said, He honored our faith and blessed us.

It's been years since I've hunted for Coke bottles. Because of my obedience to God and His Word, I am a blessed man today. The Bible says we are to be followers of those who through faith and patience inherit the promises (see Hebrews 6:12). We should never be critical of people who are inheriting the promises; we should find out what they are doing and then follow their example. That's exactly what I did the first time I heard Kenneth Copeland preach the message of faith at my church in 1969.

Carolyn and I lived in Shreveport at the time, and Brother Copeland lived in Fort Worth. But when he would come and preach, I'd get a copy of his message on tape (we had reel-to-reel tapes back then), and I would listen to the message day and night. Before I started listening to him, I knew nothing about my covenant with God and nothing about faith. Both were news to me; however, the moment I heard Brother Copeland's message, I knew it was from God.

I pursued the Word of God with everything in me. I didn't "play church" like a lot of people who heard the same message of faith back in 1969. Not me. I wanted God's best. If God said I could have something, I wanted it. My attitude was, *if God doesn't want me to be blessed, then He shouldn't have said so in His Word.* Once I found a promise in God's Word, I went after it with the tenacity of a bulldog.

As I continued to listen to Brother Copeland's teaching, I learned how to release my faith, how to trust God, how to stand—and having done all to stand, to stand therefore. Although I was able to follow Brother Copeland only through his teaching tapes at the time, I nonetheless followed the example he and Gloria had set in inheriting the promises of God through faith and patience. In time I did meet Brother Copeland, and I eventually went to work for him. When Carolyn and I moved to Fort Worth, I had the opportunity to be around him and observe him almost 24/7.

I went with Brother Copeland every time he traveled in those early days, and I listened to every word he preached in the three services he conducted daily. As soon as he finished preaching a message, I'd take the master recording to my hotel room and duplicate the recording on other reel-to-reel tapes, which I would sell at the next service.

Every time Brother Copeland taught the Word of Faith, I listened carefully and always took notes. Then I'd hear the message again in my room as I duplicated the tapes. That message was the last thing I heard before I went to bed at night.

I heard some of Brother Copeland's messages so many times that if he had stopped in the middle of a service and said, "Jerry, take over," I'd have known exactly what to say. Years later he actually did ask me to take over several times, and I preached the message just the way he would have, including using his examples.

What was I doing at that time in my life? I was following someone who through faith and patience was inheriting the promises of God. But there came a time when the Lord said, "Okay, Son, now this needs to become your revelation and not just something you heard Kenneth Copeland say." The Lord proceeded to speak various truths to my heart He wanted me to share with others. I remember the first time Brother Copeland heard me preach a particular message and he was sitting about ten feet away from me when I said something I'd learned from God. He jumped up and said, "Boy, why didn't you tell me that a long time ago? I didn't know that!" What happened? The Word of Faith had come alive in my heart. I was no longer just saying something I'd heard Brother Copeland say or something I'd heard Oral Roberts or Kenneth Hagin say. I thank God for those men who introduced me to the Word of Faith, but now it was my own revelation. And once something becomes revelation to us, nobody can take it away.

I've had people ask me many times over recent years, "Why do you think so many people have let go of the Word of Faith?" My response is that it was never a revelation to them to begin with. Had it been a revelation, they would never have let it go. They just heard something that tickled their ears, and they grabbed hold of it for a season.

Remember what Jesus said about the Word: *"The sower sows the word. And these are the ones by the wayside where the word is sown. When they hear, Satan comes immediately and takes away the word that was sown in their hearts"* (Mark 4:14–15). When Carolyn and I heard the Word of Faith, we determined the enemy would not take it from us; we refused to let it go. The Word of Faith was the best thing we'd ever heard in our lives, and after more than fifty years, it is still working for us, causing us to inherit the promises of God.

I've been preaching the Word of Faith since 1969, and I'm not about to change my message. Just as a farmer uses a combine to reap the harvest of his crops, so we use our faith to reap the kind of harvest that allows us to inherit the promises of God, which, in turn, allows us to be a blessing to others.

### We Are to Be a Blessing

Every farmer knows he cannot reap a harvest without first sowing a seed. Reaping only after sowing is a natural law established by God. Likewise, God's spiritual law also requires the sowing of seed before the reaping of a harvest.

Once a seed is sown, it's up to us to water the seed with our words, that is, the Word of God. The Word of God assures us that we are prosperous, highly favored, and blessed—but we are the ones who are responsible to sow the seed. To confess prosperity and blessing without sowing a seed is like walking around your car and confessing that it's a good car and will take you where you want to go, without first putting gasoline in the tank and then getting inside and starting the engine.

The Bible says, *And my God shall supply all your need according to His riches in glory by Christ Jesus* (Philippians 4:19). But when we back up and read the text preceding this verse, we discover the theme is sowing. Paul was writing to his partners in Philippi, those who supported his ministry financially. Inspired by the Holy Spirit, Paul wrote this letter to those who were sowers. Again, there's no harvest without first sowing seed.

In his letter to the church in Galatia, Paul said, *Let him that us taught in the word communicate unto him that teacheth in all good things* (Galatians 6:6 KJV). Another word for communicate is "support." It means "to partner with; to give." Paul goes on to say, *Do not be deceived, God is not mocked; for whatever a man sows, that he will also reap. For he who sows to the flesh will of the flesh reap corruption, but he who sows to the Spirit will of the Spirit everlasting life. And let us not grow weary while doing good, for in due season we shall reap if we do not lose heart. Therefore, as we have opportunity, let us do good to all, especially to those who are of the household of faith* (verses 7–10). To do good is a reference to being a blessing to others, which is the purpose of the harvest.

We are to be sensitive to opportunities to sow into the lives of others. I've learned that opportunities come our way every day, and these opportunities do not exclude nonbelievers, for the Bible says we are to do good to all. The good we do to others isn't limited to giving them money. We do good with a thoughtful act, a kind word, or an encouraging smile. When we walk up to someone and say, "I'm standing with you, my friend. Don't give up," we are sowing a seed. If we know this person is believing for finances, we can bless the person in a practical way as well.

On the other hand, knowing people who are sensitive to opportunities to do good does not give us the right to corner them. I remember preaching on the laws of prosperity at a meeting one night. After the service I returned to my hotel and went to sleep—until my phone rang at three o'clock in the morning. "Is this Jerry Savelle?" the female caller asked.

"Yes," I said, wondering who would be calling me at this hour.

"God told me you were going to pay off the mortgage on my house. I'm downstairs in the lobby right now, and I'll wait until you come down."

I thought, *This is news to me,* and then I said, "If God had told me to pay off someone's mortgage, I would already have done so. I learned a long time ago to be quick to obey. But, ma'am, He didn't say anything to me about this."

She said, "Well, are you listening to Him?"

"No, not really. I was asleep until you woke me up. But I do have a word from the Lord for you," I said.

"What is it?" she asked.

"Go home!"

We can't force people into meeting our needs; this is not how faith works. The Word says we are to look for opportunities to do good, to sow into the lives of all, especially to those of the household of faith.

The Amplified version of Galatians 6:10 says, *Be mindful to be a blessing.* One of the first books Carolyn wrote was titled *Born to Be a Blessing.* When we are mindful to be a blessing, we get up in the morning and say, "Lord, I want to be a blessing to somebody. Lead me, guide me, and direct my steps today." The Bible says, *The steps of a good man are ordered by the Lord* (Psalms 37:23); therefore, we can be assured He will reveal opportunities to be a blessing to others. Such opportunities have happened to me in many different ways at many different times.

For instance, one time I was in a grocery store checkout line when the person in front of me began to count pennies, apparently in hopes there were enough to pay for the few items they wanted to purchase. When they told the cashier to put an item back because they didn't have enough money, I said, "No, go ahead and keep it. Let me buy it for you."

They looked at me in surprise and said, "But you don't even know me."

"That makes it even better. You're in the Bible; you are one of the 'all men' I am supposed to bless!"

Carolyn and I do things like this all the time; it's fun. We don't wear signs around our necks that say, WE'RE BLESSED. ANYBODY NEED ANYTHING? No, we listen to the Spirit of God and follow His direction. The Message translation of Galatians 6:10 says, *Every time you get a chance, be a blessing; however, most Christians don't think this way. Most Christians prefer only to be the recipient of a blessing.*

As His disciples were looking for a place where they could prepare for the Passover, Jesus prophesied, *"Behold, when you have entered the city, a man will meet you carrying a pitcher of water; follow him to the house which he enters. Then he will show you a large, furnished upper room; there make ready"* (Luke 22:10, 12). Sadly, most people today are looking for the man with the pitcher, but they don't want to *be* the man with the pitcher.

If we read the entire story about the man with the pitcher, we find, not only was he a divine connection, but also he met the need of the disciples and of Jesus. Although the man didn't know it, the prophetic word spoken over him came to pass as Jesus prepared to fulfill His role in behalf of all mankind—the role of the Lamb of God.

But this was not the first prophetic word Jesus had spoken in accordance with the prophecies spoken about Him.

> Now when they drew near Jerusalem, and came to Bethphage, at the Mount of Olives, then Jesus sent two disciples, saying to them, "Go into the village opposite you, and immediately you will find a donkey tied, and a colt with her. Loose them and bring them to Me. And if anyone says anything to you, you shall say, 'The Lord has need of them,' and immediately he will send them."
> All this was done that it might be fulfilled which was spoken by the prophet, saying: "Tell the daughter of Zion, 'Behold, your King is coming to you, lowly, and sitting on a donkey, a colt, the foal of a donkey'" (Matthew 21:1–5).

As Jesus had prophesied, the disciples found the donkey and her colt. When the animals' owner released them to the disciples, he had no idea that, just as with the man with the pitcher, he was fulfilling a prophecy that had been spoken over him. He too was an instrument God used to meet a need in the life of Jesus as He lived out the prophecies spoken over Him.

When we understand that the purpose of God's blessing is to bring in a great harvest of both souls and the resources it takes to win those souls, then we can prepare for the harvest. And as we look for opportunities to be a blessing to others, to sow into the lives of others, we can be assured we will experience the abundant harvest God has promised in His Word.

# CHAPTER 9
## Positioned for Abundant Harvest

The way Carolyn and I lived in the early days of our marriage is the polar opposite of the way we live today. In those early days our house was furnished with items handed down by others, and as I mentioned previously, I had to collect Coke bottles for grocery money. There is absolutely no comparison between the lifestyle of lack we experienced then and the lifestyle of blessing we enjoy today. This amazing transformation came about as a result of our applying faith to the biblical principles we learned from people such as Kenneth Copeland, Oral Roberts, Kenneth Hagin, and other great Word of Faith preachers.

I've been asked many times what the greatest spiritual law I've ever learned is. Without hesitation I can say it's the law of seedtime and harvest. I was once in such deep debt, both in my personal life and in my business, I could see no natural way of ever getting out. But when I began to understand the law of seedtime and harvest, I *gave* my way out of debt, and I *gave* my way out of lack.

Carolyn and I couldn't give a hundred dollars, much less a thousand dollars, so we started with a nickel, a quarter, or a dollar. But once we made the commitment to sow in obedience to the Word, God's grace took over: *And God is able to make all grace abound toward you, that you, always having all sufficiency in all things, may have an abundance for every good work* (2 Corinthians 9:8). This is God's promise to sowers.

The Amplified Bible says, *And [God] Who provides seed for the sower and bread for eating will also provide and multiply your [resources for] sowing* (verse 10). I use this verse as the basis for a prayer I pray all the time: "Lord, continue to increase my resources for sowing." I pray this because I'm always looking for opportunities to sow; I purpose to be sensitive for these opportunities that God brings my way. In fact, prior to the beginning of the current year, I made commitments to several individuals and ministries to send a specific amount of money in the first quarter to advance their visions. The total amount of my commitment required that God increase my resources for sowing—and I can tell you He didn't let me down.

God's Word promises He will provide seed to the sower. I've made this statement many times over the years: I will never be without seed, because I'm a sower. There are times when I don't have everything I need to meet the need at hand; however, I'm never without the seed that will produce the harvest required to meet that need. My obedience to the law of seedtime and harvest puts me in control of my financial destiny. Faithful, consistent, and diligent sowers are always positioned for abundant harvest.

The Bible says, *Cast your bread upon the waters, for you will find it after many days* (Ecclesiastes 11:1). The Message translation says, *Be generous: Invest in acts of charity. Charity yields high returns.* This advice is better than anything we might hear from EF Hutton or Wall Street. The Bible assures us that *the one who blesses others is abundantly blessed* (Proverbs 11:25 MSG). The Amplified Bible says that the generous will increase more and more, and be enriched. To be *enriched* implies becoming richer and wealthier than before. Simply put, those who demonstrate charity, liberality, and blessing will increase more and more because they are positioned for the abundant harvest.

We know the abundant harvest is God's will for us; we have His prophetic word about the matter. But it is up to us to position ourselves for the abundant harvest. Charles Capps was a farmer who became a well-known teacher of the Word of Faith. He and his wife, Peggy, were friends of Carolyn's and mine.

Charles was a man who knew how to position himself for abundant harvest. He often said, "If you're down to your last one-dollar bill, do not spend it. Don't eat your seed—sow it!" The primary way we position ourselves for abundant harvest is through our abundant sowing, when and where the Lord directs.

There's no denying that the abundant harvest belongs to generous, liberal sowers. God's Word says so, and He's not a man that He should lie. Looking again to 2 Corinthians 9, we find these words: *Remember: A stingy planter gets a stingy crop; a lavish planter gets a lavish crop* (verse 6 MSG). Make the decision right now to become a lavish giver. Don't be like those who have said to me literally hundreds of times over the past fifty years, "Yes, Brother Jerry, I'll become a lavish giver—the minute my ship comes in." Most people who say this have never sent a ship out in the first place. They want to wait until conditions are perfect before they sow; however, the Word of God has this to say about such people:

> If the clouds are full of rain, they empty themselves upon the earth; and if a tree falls to the south or north, in the place where the tree falls, there it shall lie. He who observes the wind will not sow, and he who regards the clouds will not reap.
>
> As you do not know what is the way of the wind, or how the bones grow in the womb of her who is with child, so you do not know the works of God who makes everything. In the morning sow your seed, and in the evening do not withhold your hand; for you do not know which will prosper, either this or that, or whether both alike will be good (Ecclesiastes 11:3–6).

The Bible says, *God can pour on the blessings in astonishing ways so that you're ready for anything and everything, more than just ready to do what needs to be done* (2 Corinthians 9:8 MSG). Sounds to me as if this verse falls into the category of marvels, wonders, and extraordinary manifestations of God's greatness. The word astonishing means "so surprisingly impressive as to stun or to overwhelm." In other words, the God of covenant wonders can—and will—pour out blessings in astonishing ways for those who put themselves in position for abundant harvest.

While abundant sowing opens the door to the harvest, I want to share two keys to positioning ourselves for the abundant harvest. First, we must be willing to work with our hands. Second, we must be open to hearing and obeying the Rhema Word of God.

**Be Willing to Work with Our Hands**

Most of us are familiar with the Deuteronomy 28 blessings pronounced on those who would pay heed to the voice of God and obey His commandments. But I want to call particular attention to verse 12: *The Lord will open to you His good treasure, the heavens, to give the rain to your land in its season, and to bless all the work of your hand.* God promised to bless the work of our hands, which may be why the psalmist said, *And establish the work of our hands for us; yes, establish the work of our hands* (Psalms 90:17).

One time I was preaching in a meeting at Victory Christian Center in Tulsa, Oklahoma. After the evening service a man came up to me and said, "Brother Jerry, I know you're a classic-car enthusiast and you still enjoy restoring those cars."

"That's right," I said.

"Well, I have a 1957 Thunderbird I'm going to sell because I need a financial miracle. The car needs some work, but I'm going to sell it for less than its value because I need $5,000. If you're willing to buy this car for $5,000, it would help me greatly," he said.

I agreed to purchase the car for $5,000, and although it wasn't a numbers-match car, meaning the engine and transmission numbers match the last six digits of the vehicle identification number, it was still a good purchase. The work required to increase its value was something I could do myself. After putting another $2,500 into the Thunderbird, I sold it for $25,000. The Lord indeed blessed the work of my hands, and He did so in an astonishing way.

The abundant harvest sometimes comes when God arranges for us to do something in line with our expertise. God knew I had expertise in restoring classic automobiles, so He gave me the opportunity to put my hand to work and make $25,000 after I sold it. I sent the man who'd sold me the T-bird another $5000, *which produced yet another harvest for me in an astounding way.*

God is able to make every blessing come to us in abundance, including blessing the work of our hands in astonishing ways—ways that surprise, impress, and overwhelm us.

In short, whether God blesses us through the work of our hands, or some other way, He is able to do so in astonishing ways—ways that surprise, impress, and overwhelm us.

**The Rhema Word of God**

The second key to positioning ourselves for the abundant harvest has to do with our hearing and obeying the Rhema Word of God—a word spoken for our direction. We see this principle in action in the following familiar story from the book of Luke:

> So it was, as the multitude pressed about Him to hear the word of God, that He stood by the Lake of Gennesaret, and saw two boats standing by the lake; but the fishermen had gone from them and were washing their nets. Then He got into one of the boats, which was Simon's, and asked him to put out a little from the land. And He sat down and taught the multitudes from the boat.
>
> When He had stopped speaking, He said to Simon, "Launch out into the deep and let down your nets for a catch."

But Simon answered and said to Him, "Master, we have toiled all night and caught nothing; nevertheless at Your word I will let down the net." And when they had done this, they caught a great number of fish, and their net was breaking. So they signaled to their partners in the other boat to come and help them. And they came and filled the boats, so that they began to sink. When Simon Peter saw it, he fell down at Jesus' knees, saying, "Depart from me, for I am a sinful man, O Lord!"

For he and all who were with him were astonished at the catch of fish which they had taken (Luke 5:1-9).

I want to make three points about this story: First, Peter's abundant harvest was directly related to his willingness to work with his hands in his area of expertise. Second, Jesus spoke the Rhema Word of God to Peter, telling him exactly where to lower his nets. Peter's choice to listen and obey resulted in an abundant harvest. Third, all who were with him were astonished at the catch of fish. Sounds to me like they witnessed a marvel, wonder, and an extraordinary manifestation of God's greatness.

You may say, "Wait a minute, Brother Jerry, how could Peter reap an abundant harvest if he never first sowed a seed?" But he did sow a seed. Jesus had need of a boat. When Peter loaned the Lord his boat, that boat was Peter's seed. When Jesus later said, "Launch out into the deep and let down your nets for a catch," that Rhema Word of God became Peter's key to a miracle breakthrough.

If the Lord hadn't asked Peter to use his boat, Peter would have gone home and missed out on an abundant harvest. But when Jesus spoke the Rhema Word of God into Peter's particular situation, Peter's obedience triggered the miracle-breakthrough harvest he needed.

Peter's willingness to sow a seed in response to a need, set in motion activity in the Spirit realm that apparently involved the angels in a roundup of fish, the likes of which had never before been seen in the local fishing industry. Their nets began to break, and their boats began to sink as these experienced fishermen were astonished at their catch. The Message translation says they were *overwhelmed,* and the Amplified Bible says they were gripped with *bewildering amazement.*

The point I want to make is this: when we sow a seed, we need to listen to God! Like Peter, we may have expertise in a particular area—but Jesus knows even more than we do about our areas of expertise. Willingness to work with our hands or to use our training in a particular field for the purpose of reaping a harvest is necessary; however, the Rhema Word of God will direct us to the abundant harvest. The Rhema Word will position us to experience the marvels, wonders, and extraordinary manifestations of God's greatness in our lives that come as a result of our sowing a seed.

I was back in my ministry office for the first day following a series of meetings, and as I walked down the hallway, I saw my staff accountant, Carol, coming toward me. "Oh, Brother Jerry, you're just who I'm looking for," she said with a smile. "I wanted to show you the $100,000 gift we received in the mail today." She told me who the gift was from and showed me the check.

I recognized the name on the check as one of my partners, so I laid my hands on it and prayed for the person. Then I looked at Carol and said, "You know what to do with it."

She said, "Yes, sir, I'll do it."

*Jerry Savelle Ministries International* is a tithing ministry; therefore, the first ten percent of everything we receive goes into a tithe account. We use these funds to bless other ministries and to fund their projects as God directs. I thanked Carol and walked down the hallway to an exit door, but when I put my hand on the door handle I heard the Lord say, "Would you like extraordinary results from your sowing?"

"You know I would," I answered.

"Then put the entire $100,000 into the tithe account," He said.

I turned around and went directly to the accounting office and said, "Carol, hold on. Don't put $10,000 into the tithe account—put in the entire $100,000. I'll pray and ask the Lord what He wants me to do with it, and I'll call you in a little while." Then I left and went to my office to pray.

Now we needed that $100,000; we had a dozen projects that money could have been used for. But I was looking for marvels, wonders, and extraordinary manifestations. I prayed for only a short time before the Lord told me what to do with that money. I called Carol and told her what the Lord had directed me to do, so she wrote the check and immediately put it in the mail.

In the next month, we'd received three more offerings in the amount of $100,000 each. The ministry had received checks in this amount before—but we'd never received three of them within that period of time. I believe this happened because the Rhema Word of God directed me to sow the first $100,000 check we received.

Please understand, I'm not saying the same is going to happen to you. My point is that when you hear and obey the Rhema Word of God regarding your seed, you'll be positioned for the abundant harvest God has prepared for you.

That's what happened to Peter when he sowed what appeared to be an unreasonable seed. He'd been fishing without results all night, and he wanted to go home, yet he was willing to sow an unreasonable seed. When Jesus spoke the Rhema Word of God, directing Peter to launch into the deep and let down his nets, he said, *"Nevertheless, at Your word I will let down the net"* (Luke 5:5). The Amplified Bible says, *But on the ground of Your word, I will lower the nets [again],* and the Phillips translation says, *"But if you say so, I'll let the nets down."*

Peter's obedience to the Rhema Word of God positioned him for an abundant harvest. We see the same principle in operation when Isaac sowed in famine and reaped a hundredfold harvest (see Genesis 26). And when the widow woman sowed the last of her food to the prophet Elijah, her seed produced an abundant harvest (see 1 Kings 17). None of the conditions were favorable for these people, but after sowing their seed, they each heard the Rhema Word of God.

Keep sowing seed—don't ever stop sowing—but after you've sown, listen for the Rhema Word of God. Jesus will tell you what to do to position yourself for marvels, wonders, and extraordinary manifestations of God's greatness—which always produce an *abundant harvest.*

In the previous chapter I talked about the importance of watering our seed with the word of God coming ouf of our mouths. I want to share with you some of the scripture verses I use to water my seeds. Each verse is followed by my declaration.

**Prophetic Declarations for Abundant Harvest**

*"While the earth remains, seedtime and harvest ... shall not cease"*(Genesis 8:22). I sow my seeds in faith, knowing that the law of seedtime and harvest is working in my behalf.

*"The kingdom of God is as if a man should scatter seed on the ground ... and the seed should sprout and grow"* (Mark 4:26-27). I expect every seed I have sown to grow up, to spring up, and to produce and abundant harvest.

*If they obey and serve Him, they shall spend their days in prosperity, and their years in pleasure* (Job 36:11). Because I have been obedient to God and I have sown my seeds, I fully expect my days to be filled with prosperity and my years with pleasures.

*The Lord hath been mindful of us: he will bless us. The Lord shall increase you more and more, you and your children* (Psalms 115:12, 14 KJV). Because God has seen my sowing and His mind is continually on me, I'm expecting more and more financial blessings and more and more increase to come into my life.

*"Give, and it will be given to you: good measure, pressed down, shaken together, and running over will be put into your bosom. For with the same measure that you use, it will be measured back to you"* (Luke 6:38). I expect good measure, pressed down, shaken together, and running over on every harvest for every seed I've sown.

*He who sows bountifully will also reap bountifully* (2 Corinthians 9:6). I'm entitled to, and I'm expecting, a bountiful harvest because I'm a bountiful sower.

*And God is able to make all grace abound toward you, that you, always having all sufficiency in all things, may have an abundance for every good work* (2 Corinthians 9:8). I expect to have all sufficiency, more than enough, abounding in financial blessing, so that I'm able to sow into every good work the Holy Spirit impresses me to bless.

*"Believe in the Lord your God, and you shall be established; believe His prophets, and you shall prosper"* (2 Chronicles 20:20). I believe in the Lord my God, and I believe what His prophet has spoken regarding my season of abundant harvest; therefore, I expect this harvest every day of my life.

The Word of God says, *"Who is like You, O Lord, among the gods? Who is like You, glorious in holiness, fearful in praises, doing*

*wonders?* (Exodus 15:11). The Message translation says, *Who compares with you among gods, O God?* Who compares with you in power, in holy majesty, in awesome praises, wonder-working God? Our God is a wonder-working God!

The Bible says, *"He does great things past finding out, yes, wonders without number"* (Job 9:10). The Message translation says, *His miracle-surprises can't be counted.* And the psalmist said, *You are the God who does wonders; You have declared Your strength among the peoples* (Psalms 77:14).

Psalms 100:4 tells us that we are *to enter into His gates with thanksgiving, and into His courts with praise.* Psalms 135:1 declares, *Praise the Lord! Praise the name of the Lord: praise Him, O you servants of the Lord!* The depth of our praise will determine the magnitude of our harvest.

As you continue to praise God for His faithfulness to His Word, my prayer for you is that God will continually surprise you and cause you to stand in amazement at the astounding ways He brings about abundant harvest for you. I declare that marvels, wonders, and extraordinary manifestations of God's greatness will be commonplace in your life—in the name of Jesus!

# THE AUTHOR

Dr. Jerry Savelle was an average, blue-collar man who was struggling and needed God's help. While he considered himself a "nobody," when he became a believer God told him not to worry about it because He was a master at making champions out of nobodies. God has since taken Dr. Savelle from being a constant quitter to a man who knows how to stand on the Word of God until victory is experienced. Because of the life-changing combination of God's faithfulness and Dr. Savelle's "no quit" attitude, his life is totally different than it was forty-nine years ago.

Since 1969, Dr. Savelle has been traveling the world teaching people how to win in life. Dr. Savelle has ministered in more than thirty-five hundred churches in thirty-six nations, and has overseas offices in the United Kingdom, Australia, Canada, and South Africa as well as numerous Bible Schools all over the world.

God has used Dr. Savelle to impact people all over the world who are burned out on religion and who have backslidden in their walk with God, as well as Christians who have a need to hear the Word of God presented in terms applicable to their lives, dreams, and destinies. He is the host of the Jerry Savelle Ministries television broadcast which airs in two hundred countries worldwide.

Dr. Savelle is the author of more than seventy books, including his bestsellers, If Satan Can't Steal Your Joy, He Can't Keep Your Goods and Called to Battle, Destined to Win. He and his wife, Carolyn, also serve as founding Pastors of Heritage of Faith Christian Center in Crowley, Texas.

# Further Resources

For additional products, including books, audios and videos, visit **www.jerrysavelle.org**

**JSMI HEADQUARTERS**
P.O. Box 748
Crowley, TX. USA 76036
817.297.3155
www.JerrySavelle.org

**JSMI AUSTRALIA/ASIA**
63 Township Drive
West Burleigh, QLD
+617.5576.5534
JSMI@JSMIAustralia.org

**JSMI CANADA**
P.O. Box 700
Lambeth Station
London, Ontario
N6P1W4
+519.652.1611
Canada@JSMI.org

**JSMI AFRICA**
P.O. Box 13899
Leraatsfontein 1038
South Africa
+27 13 697 2476

**JSMI EUROPE**
4 Hanley House, Tidenham
Chepstow,
NP16 7NA, UK
+(44)01291 628074
JSMIEurope@aol.com